Email Marketing Demystified

Praise for *Email Marketing Demystified*

"I've done email marketing for over a decade and have interviewed over 1,000 entrepreneurs about how they built their businesses, and I still learned a lot about growing an email list from *Email Marketing Demystified*. What sets it apart is that Matthew does not give empty theories. He shows actionable techniques that he used to build a 200k+ mailing list and includes examples of how he used those techniques."

Andrew Warner
Founder and CEO, Mixergy
Mixergy.com

"Matthew has already walked the walk with email marketing, and now he's committed his knowledge to paper. Recommended."

Rob Walling
Co-Founder, Drip
GetDrip.com

"Matthew provides a step-by-step process that makes email marketing approachable and accessible to entrepreneurs at all levels. If you are just getting started with email or you already have a mailing list of 10,000 subscribers, *Email Marketing Demystified* can help grow your business through the power of email marketing."

Jaime Tardy
Founder, Eventual Millionaire
EventualMillionaire.com

"Email marketing is an incredibly valuable marketing channel. I do it in my business, but I know I could be doing it a lot better. *Email Marketing Demystified* is a deep dive into the trenches of effective email marketing that shows what actually works. I found the book to be easy to digest and came away with some great takeaways that are immediately applicable to my business."

John T. Meyer
Co-Founder, Lemonly
Lemonly.com

"With so many new options in social media, it seems some current marketers put more emphasis on techniques for selling rather than on creating value and true service. In this book, Matthew gives step-by-step practices to grow exponentially by giving massive value while honoring the time proven principles of integrity and wowing our customers. I expect this book to add $1 million in new revenue to our business this year."

Dan Miller
New York Times bestselling author of
48 Days to the Work You Love
48Days.com

"If you have any doubt about the power of email marketing, *Email Marketing Demystified* will quickly dispel them. In the book, Matthew lays out an easy to implement step-by-step plan to create your own email marketing system that actually works! This book is a must-read for any entrepreneur that runs an online business and is prepared to IGNITE!"

John Lee Dumas
Host, EntrereneurOnFire
EntrepreneurOnFire.com

'I've known Matt for several years now and watched him build several semi-automated businesses that created hundreds of thousands of dollars (and now into the millions) quickly. A little story: I shared with Matt an email "having a sale" sequence that I thought would quickly add 30% or more in revenue when one of his businesses was still under six figures. Instead of 30% growth he turned it into around 300% growth in a year. Listen to Matt when it comes to email for building a company fast. Read *Email Marketing Demystified* and follow Matt's step-by-step plan and you too can grow your business rapidly."

Tim Conley
TimConley.co

"*Email Marketing Demystified* is packed with real-world-tested strategies, tips and tricks only a veteran of email marketing would know. If you are new to email marketing, Matt's detailed, step-by-step methods will cut your learning curve by years and allow you to start monetizing that portion of your business immediately. Even as an experienced email marketer, I found gems I implemented into my own business that have help me grow my subscribers more quickly. Matt has a knack for thinking of ways to grow and monetize an email list that you probably never considered!"

Tim Bourqui
Co-founder, After Offers
AfterOffers.com

Email Marketing Demystified

Build a Massive Mailing List, Write Copy that Converts and Generate More Sales

By Matthew Paulson

Dedication

To my son Micah, I love you more than anything in the world. You provide all of the hope, inspiration, and joy that I need to get up early every day and continue to grow my businesses.

To my wife Karine, thank you for continuing to support and encourage me in everything I do. Thank you for not shaking your head at me whenever I come up with a crazy new business idea, and thank you for allowing me the opportunity to provide for our family in unique and creative ways. Most importantly, thank you for being my best friend.

Table of Contents

Foreword

by John McIntyre

"But John, isn't email marketing dead?" Dave asked.

I sighed.

It was 11:30am on a sunny Tuesday, and I was checking my email at Suvarnabhumi International Airport in Bangkok, Thailand.

I was en route to the U.S. to speak at a conference on the power email marketing has to make sales and revenue explode.

I had to laugh at the irony.

I had built a profitable business with email marketing, which generated 100% of its profits from email marketing, yet I was repeatedly being told by people like Dave that email marketing was dead.

These people were smart business owners who just didn't get it. They thought email marketing was a waste of time.

That it didn't work.

That it made people want to punch their computer.

Who could blame them?

We've been told "email marketing is dead" for years.

According to the "experts," no one checks email anymore. They've all moved over to Facebook, Twitter, Pinstagram, Instarest, or whatever the latest social network is called.

Plus, most of us consider checking email to be a "necessary evil." We don't check email because we love it. We check it because we have to. We'd rather be checking how many likes our latest post on Facebook received.

But as business owners, our personal relationship with our inbox is not indicative of whether email marketing works or not.

Like every great marketer, Matt cares more about data than human emotion, and that's why he begins *Email Marketing Demystified* by describing what the data says.

As it turns out, the data tells a *very* different story than what we've all heard.

Did you know that a study from the Direct Marketing Association found that businesses earn an average of $43.00 for every $1.00 invested in email marketing?

In other words, email marketing is *proven* to produce a 4,300% return on investment (ROI).

In the same study, not only did email marketing deliver a whopping 4,300% ROI, but it also beat every single other advertising channel, including social media, search engine optimization, and direct mail.

Email marketing is not dead. Not even close.

But that's not all...

If marketing channels were cars, even the best social media and SEO campaigns would be like a Mercedes Benz—fast and luxurious, but certainly not the best in their class—while email marketing would be a McLaren F1 or a Lamborghini Gallardo.

Email marketing doesn't just beat everything else. It leaves them in the dust.

And so, I have a question for you:

Have YOU implemented an email marketing strategy yet?

If you have, are you optimizing it, improving it, and always striving to make it better?

If you aren't, you are making a *huge* mistake.

Depending on the size of your business, you could be leaving hundreds of thousands of dollars on the table. Maybe even millions.

All because you haven't taken the time to implement an effective email marketing strategy.

Well, it's time for that to change.

When it comes to email marketing and learning how to generate a 4,300% ROI, I can't think of anyone I'd rather learn from than Matt Paulson.

Why?

Because unlike other so-called "experts," Matt lives and breathes email marketing. He is a bonafide expert.

One of his businesses is a financial newsletter which goes out to more than 250,000 investors on a daily basis.

Marketing books usually present ideas from some "fly by night" wantrapreneur who has never achieved anything substantial.

But that's not what you're going to get with *Email Marketing Demystified*.

Instead, you're going to get email marketing strategies from someone who knows how to apply them to wildly different businesses in totally different markets.

As a successful serial entrepreneur with a growing multimillion-dollar empire built largely on the back of the email marketing strategies you're about to learn, Matt is the *real deal*.

By now, I'm hoping that you're ready to generate a 4,300% ROI in your business (and you're ready to let someone as smart, successful, and savvy as Matt help you do it).

So let's talk specifics:

What are you going to learn in *Email Marketing Demystified*?

First, you'll get the low-down on the best email service providers for your business, including which companies offer the best features for the best price (and which will burn a hole in your pocket without offering you much in return).

Next, you'll discover the art and science of getting people to sign up for your email list on your website, including how to create a killer lead magnet that stops even your coldest prospects dead in their tracks and makes them sign up. Plus, you'll also find out exactly which type of opt-in forms to add to your website for maximum conversions (and how to craft the perfect message that communicates to your ideal prospect's deepest desires).

Now comes the part most people dread... creating the email campaigns. However, you have nothing to worry about because Matt explains how writing amazing emails can be easy, simple, and fast. This is where you'll learn the ins and outs of creating email campaigns that are opened, clicked, and bought time and time again.

Plus, Matt even does a deep-dive on copywriting (one of my favorite topics) and shows you how to write blockbuster emails on command.

Once you have your email software, lead magnet, email opt-ins, and various campaigns, you'll get to the most exciting step in the book: Monetization (in other words, how to make money with your email list).

In this section, Matt goes into all the various ways you can generate revenue from your email list (he even surprised me with a few methods of monetization that I wasn't aware of).

When it comes to monetizing your email list, selling your own products and services is the most common method, but it is far from the only method. Matt also covers co-registration advertising, selling another company's products, and running newsletter ads. He also explains how you can rent out your email list to other companies (this is perfect for a business that has an email list but no products of their own to sell).

After monetization, you'll jump into the dark, murky area of the legal side of email marketing. When does email marketing become spam? How can you avoid breaking the law while also serving your customers by selling your products and services?

Once you've made it through the boring-but-totally-necessary legal aspects of email marketing, Matt hits you with some killer tips on how to avoid the spam box and promotions tab; how to maintain a good reputation with Gmail, Yahoo!, and the other email companies; and how to ensure your email campaigns get delivered every single time you send them.

The final section of this book delves into cold email outreach, also known as outbound email marketing. This topic is particularly important to my company at the moment as we are doing a lot of cold email outreach. I was glad to find several tips and tricks in this section that I'm sure will improve our results. If your business sells high-ticket products and services like mine, cold email outreach is the strategy for you.

So there you have it:

Email Marketing Demystified is the complete guide to email marketing—from getting people onto your email list, converting them into customers with amazing campaigns, managing the legal side of things, and using cold email outreach to sell high-ticket products and services.

If you'd like to see breakthrough growth in your business, read this book and follow Matt's advice to the letter. It will transform your business. You will end up with more money than ever, with more time than ever, and you will finally be able to create the lifestyle you've wanted since the day you got started in business.

I've personally experienced the amazing benefits of email marketing in my own business. I've also seen it again and again in my clients' and customers' businesses.

Email marketing works like rocket-fuel for businesses... but *only* if you implement what you learn.

So please, please, PLEASE: don't just read this book...

...take action and enjoy the incredible results (because you deserve no less than the best).

Email marketing is *not* magic, but it certainly starts to *feel* that way when you see such incredible results.

When you implement these strategies and discover that they work splendidly, please email me and let me know how it worked out for you.

I would love to hear from you.

Best of luck,

John McIntyre
The Autoresponder Guy
john@themcmethod.com | TheMcMethod.com

Best-selling author of *Email Marketing: 63 Money-Making Insights From The Wildly Popular McMethod Email Marketing Podcast.*

Medellín, Colombia
July 23, 2015

Introduction

Email is one of the most powerful and most underutilized marketing channels available on earth. It has been the primary means of electronic communication since the 1970's. Since then, numerous bulletin board services, instant messaging services, chat services, social networks, and other "email killers" have come and gone. Yet email continues to serve as the core communication platform of the Internet— and it's only growing. Between 2014 and 2018, the number of email accounts in existence worldwide is expected to grow from 4.11 billion to 5.23 billion. Currently, more than 2.5 billion people, or 35% of the world's population, have access to email, and more than 100 billion emails are sent and received every day of the year.[1]

Despite the widespread use of the digital juggernaut that is email, many entrepreneurs have yet to implement an effective email marketing strategy in their business because they don't know how to do it or haven't recognized how powerful of a marketing channel email can be. *Email Marketing Demystified* hopes to change that by providing a step-by-step guide for any business (or nonprofit) to leverage the power of email marketing.

Why Email Marketing?

Email provides you the opportunity to send a message to your audience for any purpose on any day of the year at effectively no cost to you. This is an incredibly powerful communication channel. When you do email marketing well and send the right messages to the right people at the right time, you are certain to build an audience of highly-engaged fans that can't wait for your next message to hit their inboxes. Additionally, they are ready to buy whenever you have a product or service to promote.

There are several compelling reasons that your business should adopt email as a marketing channel:

- **Email Marketing Generates Massive ROI** – A study from the Direct Marketing Association found that a business will earn an average of $43.00 for every $1.00 invested in email marketing.[2] In a study from GigaOm, marketers have consistently ranked email marketing as the single most effective strategy for generating awareness, acquiring leads, generating sales, and customer retention.[3]

- **Email Marketing Generates Long-Term Results** – MarketBeat first started collecting opt-ins in late 2010. Five years later, a good number of our subscribers that signed up during the first month continue to receive content, engage with our content, and buy products and services from our business. When you start building an email list, you are building a long-term asset that will generate revenue and social capital for your business for many years to come.

- **Most Customers Want Email from Businesses** – A study from MarketingSherpa found that 72% of U.S. consumers say email is their favorite way to communicate with the companies that they do business with. 61% of consumers reported they like to receive weekly promotional emails from their favorite brands, and 28% of consumers want to receive promotional emails more frequently.[4] Additionally, 70% of consumers say they will always open email from their favorite companies[5], and 95% of people who opted in to receive email from brands say that the marketing email they receive is either somewhat useful or very useful.[6]

- **Email Marketing Dramatically Outperforms Social Media Marketing** – A study from McKinsey & Company found that businesses are 40 times more likely to create a new customer from email marketing than they are through social media.[7] Another study found that 66% of marketers believe email marketing delivers a "good" or "excellent" ROI, while only 41% of them said they feel the same way about social media marketing.[8]

- **Email is Ubiquitous** – Nearly 87% of the population in the United States has Internet access in their home[9], and 95% of consumers use email[10]. You just don't have to worry whether or not any of your potential customers have an email address or not.

• **Email is a Resilient Technology** – Email has effectively existed in its current format since the early 1980s. That was 15 years before most homes had a personal computer and Internet access, and 25 years before the first iPhone was released. Despite the world's massive amount of technological progress and the proliferation of personal computers, smartphones, and tablets, the technical specifications for email have only been updated a handful of times in the last 30 years. While other communication technologies have come and gone, email continues to withstand the test of time. When you invest in email marketing, you know that the medium won't be replaced by a bigger and better thing a few years from now.

• **Email Marketing is Federated** – When you build an audience on Facebook, Twitter, or Pinterest, you are totally at the mercy of the whims of a company whose best interests are not aligned with yours. You could put a lot of time, energy, and money into building an audience on a particular platform only for that platform to change the rules in such a way that kills the profitability of your campaign. That will never be the case with email, because no one company has control of the technical specification for email or control over the technology infrastructure that allows email to be delivered to the world's four billion inboxes.

Email marketing continues to be one of the most effective and most resilient marketing strategies for both digital businesses and brick-and-mortar companies. It's hard to match the potential ROI offered by email marketing, and you can rest assured that your email marketing efforts will continue to generate revenue into the future.

But Isn't Email Marketing Dead?

Every now and then, a technology expert or a journalist will come out and declare the demise of email. In 2009, technology columnist John C. Dvorak argued that email is dead because of spam, competing social media platforms, security problems, and a number of other issues.[11] In January 2014, Facebook co-founder Dustin Moskovitz declared that the world had reached "peak email" and said that the business world would quickly move to other platforms.[12] Inc.com Contributing Editor John Brandon wrote in April 2015 that email would be obsolete by 2020.[13]

While claiming that email is dead or dying makes for a great headline, such claims aren't in line with reality. Email serves as the core communications platform of the Internet, and email usage is only growing. The number of worldwide users is expected to grow from 2.5 billion in 2014 to 2.8 billion by 2018.[14] Radicati expects the number of worldwide email accounts to grow by 26.8% between 2014 and 2018. Every major online service in the world, ranging from social media services like Facebook and Twitter to e-commerce stores like Amazon and Overstock, requires you to provide an email address to do business with them. Email is deeply ingrained into the fabric of the Internet and won't be brushed aside by a competing service anytime soon.

Isn't Email Marketing Spamming?

Some people who are unfamiliar with email marketing think that all types of commercial emails are spam. "Spamming" is sending the same commercial message indiscriminately to a large number of recipients without their permission. Modern email marketing is based almost entirely on first receiving someone's permission to email them. When you provide news, updates, and product information to someone that has *signed up* on your website to receive news, updates, and product information, that's not spam.

While there are a few unscrupulous email marketers that use spam as a marketing strategy, most email marketers only send email to people that have opted in to their mailing lists and have specifically asked to receive email from them. Savvy email marketers know they can generate much better business results by cultivating an audience that actually wants their content than by indiscriminately spamming their marketing material to strangers.

I Hate Marketing Email and Popup Opt-In Forms. Why Would I Want to Send Marketing Email to My Audience?

Many tech savvy people have a natural aversion to advertisements and other marketing materials. They think they are immune to being influenced by advertising and think advertisements just get in the way of their experiences using the web. They use ad-blocking plugins to remove ads from their web browser and use strict spam filters to keep unwanted messages out of their inboxes. They absolutely hate popup opt-in forms, because they think they are annoying. If it were up to them, they would never receive any kind of marketing email, because they think that it just clogs up their inboxes.

If this sounds like you, you may initially feel uncomfortable with many of the recommendations in this book. Remember that you are not your audience. Just because you don't like to receive email from brands doesn't mean your customers feel the same way. While I try to stay off most mailing lists and ensure my personal inbox is empty at the end of every day, my wife, Karine's, inbox is full of promotional email from every major clothing retailer, and she loves it. She loves getting coupons and deals and seeing what new styles are coming out. She receives at least 20 emails each day from brands, and it doesn't bother her a bit.

Not everyone uses email in the same way. You might see your email inbox as a work "to do" list that needs to be cleared out. Other email users see it as a stream of information where they can pick and choose what they want to read and ignore. If an email user loves the content that you produce, of course they will want to have that as part of the email influx they receive every day. The entire process of list building, setting up an autoresponder series, and sending broadcast emails is just a way for your audience to better engage with the content and products that you are already producing through their email stream.

Every now and then, I'll hear someone that runs a website say something like, "I hate popups and I hate marketing email. I would never use them in my business." What they're really saying is, "I hate making money," because email marketing is an incredibly effective marketing strategy. They just can't get past their personal biases against advertising to recognize the opportunity that's before them. If one of your audience members wants to get your latest content and product information through email, you should allow them to do so despite any personal misgivings you might have against seeing advertisements on the web. If someone genuinely doesn't want to receive email from you, they won't fill out an opt-in form on your website.

My Story

During the last five years, I have built four different businesses that rely heavily on email marketing. My largest business, MarketBeat.com (formerly Analyst Ratings Network), publishes a daily investment newsletter to more than 250,000 subscribers. MarketBeat is on track to generate $2.5 million in revenue in 2015, and more than $1 million of that is directly attributable to email marketing. The company sends out more than 10 million permission-based emails monthly and attracts more than 20,000 new organic opt-ins each month. The company generates revenue through subscription information products, newsletter ads, display advertising, email list rentals, and co-registration advertising.

The second business I built was called Lightning Releases (lightningreleases.com), which is a press release writing and distribution service that uses email as one of its primary marketing strategies. I started this service in 2012 as a low-cost alternative to some of the more expensive press release distribution services. For $99.00, the service allows individuals, businesses, and nonprofits the opportunity to have their press release featured in news portals like Google News, Bing News, and Topix, as well as the websites of many major national newspapers. The business generated more than $200,000 in 2014. I sold it to a couple of investors in early 2015 so that I could focus on my other projects.

The third email-driven business I helped launch is called GoGo Photo Contest (gogophotocontest.com), which helps animal shelters and humane societies raise money through donate-to-vote photo contest fundraisers. I co-founded this company in 2013 with a couple of good friends of mine, Jason and Stevie Shea. GoGo Photo Contest uses outbound email marketing to contact executive directors of animal shelters and educate them, then make them aware of how we can help their organizations raise money. The company works with approximately 150 animal welfare groups each year and has helped animal shelters across the country raise more than $1.5 million in donations between October 2013 and October 2015.

Finally, I'm a partner in a company called USGolfTV, which is a digital publishing company that produces a regionally-syndicated television show that's available in 12 million homes and 25 states. USGolfTV also produces premium video training courses that help golfers improve their game. USGolfTV was founded in 2010 by Todd Kolb and Tyler Prins. I acquired an equity stake in the company in August 2014 and was tasked with helping the business build an email list and grow its ad revenue. In the first 12 months, USGolfTV grew its email list from 5,000 subscribers to 52,000 subscribers using the strategies outlined in this book. The company also doubled its monthly average revenue in the last year.

There are many different resources that teach email marketing that are of varying degrees of quality. Some of them are written by people that don't have a lot of experience and don't really know what they're talking about. You can rest assured that this is not the case with *Email Marketing Demystified*. The information and advice written in this book comes directly from my personal experiences building MarketBeat, Lightning Releases, GoGo Photo Contest, and USGolfTV. None of the information in this book is theoretical, made-up, or unproven. Every tip, trick, and strategy in this book has been tested and proven in at least one of my businesses.

What You'll Learn in Email Marketing Demystified

Email Marketing Demystified is a comprehensive work designed to teach you every aspect of email marketing. In the first chapter, you'll learn about the necessity of having an email service provider and the different types of email service providers that exist. You'll also learn what to look for in an email service provider and decide which service is best for you.

In the second and third chapters of this book, you will learn how to collect email sign-ups. I will show you how to create a lead magnet to attract more sign-ups on your website. You will also learn which types of opt-in forms work best and how to craft your messaging to maximize the number of opt-ins you receive. These chapters will also help you discover other creative ways to grow your mailing list independently of your website.

In the fourth and fifth chapters of the book, you'll learn about welcome emails, autoresponders, broadcast emails, and other types of messages you will send to your list. These chapters will show exactly what types of email you should send to engage your audience and generate revenue. There is also a deep dive into email copywriting so that you know exactly how to write different types of messages to your list.

The sixth chapter focuses entirely on monetization, or how to make money with your mailing list. You will learn six different ways to generate revenue through your email list, including co-registration advertising, selling your company's products and services, promoting another company's products as a service, running newsletter advertisements, renting your email list, and generating traffic for your website. If you want to learn how MarketBeat generates more than $1 million per year through email marketing, read this chapter.

The seventh and eighth chapters of *Email Marketing Demystified* focus on the legal aspects of email marketing and making sure that your messages actually get delivered to your subscribers' inboxes and not in their spam folders. You will learn about the United States' CAN-SPAM legislation and Canada's anti-spam legislation (CASL) and what you need to do to stay compliant with both. You will also learn about the best practices to follow in order to maintain your reputation as an email sender and keep your domain name and IP address off blacklists.

The ninth (and final) chapter of this book explains generating sales through outbound email marketing, also known as email prospecting. Most of the book focuses on attracting subscribers and keeping them engaged with your mailing list. This chapter focuses on identifying prospective customers, introducing your business to them through a cold email, qualifying them as customers, and generating sales. If your business has a relatively small set of potential customers and sells relatively high price point products with an average order size of $500.00 or more, read this chapter first.

In the appendix, there are links to a number of other resources that will help with your effort to become a better email marketer, including books, blogs, podcasts, and educational products that are worth checking out. There are also four different case studies placed throughout the book to show you what kind of results and successes are possible through email marketing.

This book references a number of specific email marketing tools, plugins, and services you can utilize to get started quickly with your email marketing efforts, ensuring you can be confident in using reputable products and services. There are comparisons of the features and benefits of specific products. I also have a few personal product recommendations within the book, so keep an eye out for them. Please note that neither I nor my company receive any payment or any form of compensation of any kind for recommending these few products. I will only recommend a specific product or service if I truly think it is the best solution for my friends, business partners, acquaintances, and other readers of this book.

A Call to Action

Email marketing is an incredibly powerful marketing channel that will generate massive long-term results. You won't become a millionaire overnight by implementing email marketing in your business, but you will see steadily improving returns as your email list grows and your strategies mature. If you had started gathering email addresses on your website five years ago, you could have had a mailing list of tens of thousands or *hundreds* of thousands of subscribers today. You would have built a long-term asset that could continue to generate revenue for your business even if everything else implodes, because you can always create a new product, service, or other offers and promote it to your mailing list. While you can't go back in time and start your mailing list five years ago, you can do the next best thing and start growing your mailing list and implementing email marketing in your business (or your nonprofit) today.

Chapter One

Selecting an Email Service Provider (ESP)

The first step in building your email marketing empire is to put the technical infrastructure in place in order to handle the type and volume of email you will send. If you were going to set up a call center, you would never try to run it using only your personal phone number. You would hire an expert to tell you what you need, get dozens of phone lines and other telecommunications hardware, and put software in place specifically to handle routing calls. Likewise, you should never try to run an email marketing campaign using your personal email account.

A standard email account with Gmail, Outlook, or Yahoo is simply not capable of organizing and contacting large numbers of people through a mailing list. Instead, you would want to work with an email service provider (ESP) that provides specialized software and infrastructure that can help manage your mailing list and deliver email to your subscribers.

What Email Service Providers Do

An email service provider is a company that provides email marketing software and delivery infrastructure to businesses, nonprofits, and individuals.

Here are some common tasks that your ESP will handle:

- **List Management** – Your ESP will store the list of active subscribers on your mailing list(s). They will also automatically add new subscribers to your mailing list that sign up through your opt-in forms, process users that want to unsubscribe, and remove old email addresses that are no longer valid.

- **Templates** – Your ESP may offer pre-made HTML templates that will provide your email with a unique look and feel. Most ESPs also offer the ability to upload a custom HTML template created by you or a web designer that you hired. It may also offer the ability to ensure your HTML template is compatible with most major email clients.

- **Autoresponders and Mail Scheduling** – Your ESP will let you send a pre-written series of emails to all new subscribers over a period of several weeks or months. This is known as an autoresponder series. Your ESP will also allow you to create a calendar of future mailings and schedule mailings to send out at a particular date and time.

- **Delivery Engine** – Sending a large volume of email requires a significant technical infrastructure and knowledge of how email deliverability works. Your ESP will provide the servers and software needed to actually deliver your email to subscribers and can help if you ever run into a deliverability issue, such as being blacklisted.

- **Tracking** – Your ESP will be able to track important metrics related to the performance of any given email, including the total number of sends, opens, bounces, clicks, and unsubscribes. Some email service providers may also provide a tracking pixel that will allow you to tie any given sale back to a particular email.

- **Spam Testing** – Your ESP can gauge the content of each email that you send against commonly-used spam filters. You will receive an automatic warning if you use language found in many typical spam messages or make other technical mistakes that may cause an email provider to block the message or deliver it to a subscriber's spam folder.

- **Marketing Automation** – Some ESPs will allow you to send a series of messages in response to users that take a specific action, such as opting in for a new offer, purchasing a product, or abandoning their shopping cart on an e-commerce site. This functionality, known as marketing automation, allows you to send more targeted email to your subscribers and will likely improve the long-term success of your email campaign. Please note that the quality of marketing automation tools can vary widely from ESP to ESP. If marketing automation is something that you want to take advantage of, select an ESP that was built with marketing automation in mind.

- **Dynamic Messages** – Your email service provider will allow you to dynamically customize the content of each email to tailor it to each subscriber. The most common use of this functionality is to open each email with "Dear [FirstName]" instead of a generic greeting.

- **HTML and Text Formatting** – Your ESP will be able to create emails that are formatted as both HTML and plain text, which may improve your deliverability rates.

Types of Email Service Providers

Not all email service providers (ESPs) provide the same tools and functionality. There are three categories of email service providers that have different strengths, focuses, and levels of service: email infrastructure providers (EIPs), general email service providers (GESPs), and marketing automation providers (MAPs).

Email Infrastructure Providers

Email infrastructure providers (EIPs) focus primarily on the actual delivery of your email. They provide the network infrastructure and email deliverability expertise necessary to make sure that your email actually gets delivered to your subscribers' inboxes. EIPs generally do not provide list management services, templates, marketing automation, or email scheduling tools. They are primarily used by software developers that do their own list management through custom software. Often they can also be used to send transactional emails, such as welcome messages and order confirmation messages. EIP users will often schedule messages using an SMTP server or an API provided by the EIP in lieu of a web interface. Generally, you would only select an EIP over a GESP if you are writing custom marketing software or are using a piece of third-party software that requires an outside email server.

Here are some commonly used email infrastructure providers:

- AmazonSES - aws.amazon.com/ses
- Elastic Email - elasticemail.com
- Mailjet - mailjet.com
- Mandrill – mandrillapp.com
- PostMark - postmarkapp.com
- SendGrid – sendgrid.com
- Socket Labs - socketlabs.com

It is important to note that the quality of service can vary substantially between EIPs. In my experience, you get what you pay for. I had a less than desirable experience with a low-cost EIP about a year ago, and have since then moved all of my EIP mailing over to a more expensive enterprise plan with SendGrid. I haven't had any major issues since.

General Email Service Providers

Like EIPs, general email service providers (GESPs) provide the necessary network infrastructure and deliverability expertise needed to make sure that your email actually makes it to your subscribers' inboxes. GESPs will also provide all of the list management, templating, mail scheduling, performance tracking, and spam testing that ESP customers expect. If you are building a general mailing list for the purpose of sending newsletters and other content to your audience, a GESP is your best bet.

Here are some commonly used general email service providers:

- Aweber - aweber.com
- Constant Contact – constantcontact.com
- Campaign Monitor – campaignmonitor.com
- Drip – getdrip.com
- iContact - icontact.com
- GetResponse – getresponse.com
- MailChimp – mailchimp.com

Marketing Automation Platforms

Marketing automation platforms (MAPs) cater to a superset of the functionality that general email service providers offer. In addition to providing email delivery infrastructure and list management services, MAPs will provide special tools that allow you to send a specific email series to an individual subscriber based on any actions they take or tags that you assign them. For example, if a customer purchases a certain product, you might want to send them a series of emails that provide instructions to use that product. With a MAP, new customers will automatically be tagged as a purchaser of that product and will receive the email series that you set up ahead of time. When set up properly, MAPs can send more targeted and relevant email to your subscribers, which will dramatically improve the effectiveness of your email marketing campaigns.

The line between general email service providers and marketing automation platforms has blurred during the last several years. Some older GESPs have added marketing automation functionality to compete with services that were built from the ground up with marketing automation in mind. At the same time, MAPs have worked to make sure they offer the same level of list management and email delivery services offered by GESPs.

Here are some commonly used email marketing automation platforms:

- Active Campaign - activecampaign.com/automation

- Drip - getdrip.com

- Ontraport - ontraport.com

- Infusionsoft - infusionsoft.com

Purchase Considerations

When selecting an email service provider, there are several factors to consider. Here are some things to keep in mind:

- **Type of ESP** – Determine whether you need an email infrastructure provider, a general email service provider, or a marketing automation platform. Unless you are writing custom software and need to send email through an API call, your best bet is to choose one that offers high-quality list management services and advanced marketing automation tools. While you might not use marketing automation functionality when you are getting started, you will want to have it available for use later on due to the incredible value it can provide to your email marketing efforts.

- **Functionality** – Most email service providers offer a similar baseline of functionality, including list management, email delivery, templating, spam testing, and message scheduling. List any advanced features that you might want to leverage in your email marketing strategy and compare and contrast competing services to see which might offer the best combination of tools and services for your business.

- **Age of Software** – Email service providers do not age well because of a variety of software and database issues. Some older ESPs launched between 10 and 20 years ago have simply not been able to keep up with the functionality, user interface, and quality of service offered by those launched more recently. Older ESPs have to deal with massive datasets of customer information and with legacy software code, which make them difficult to upgrade over time.

- **Cost** – Pricing between ESPs can vary significantly based on your usage and the level of service provided. Use an ESP's pricing page to calculate your cost now based on your current sending level, and consider what using an ESP will cost you as your mailing list grows over time.

- **Customer Service** – Some ESPs offer much better customer service than others. If you inadvertently get added to a blacklist or have some other deliverability issue, you are going to need an ESP that has your back and can step in to help alleviate the situation. Use Google to search for customer reviews of the ESP you are considering, and also search for the company's name followed by the word "sucks" to see how many users are dissatisfied with a given service.

• **Terms and Conditions** – Some ESPs will suspend your account without warning if too many users mark your emails as spam or if you have too high of a bounce rate. Make sure you actually *read* the terms and services of the ESP you are considering and understand what circumstances are grounds for shutting down your account.

Take a considerate amount of time to research and compare email service providers before selecting your ESP. After you have started building a mailing list with an ESP, it can be very difficult to switch to another provider. A new ESP might require you to reconfirm your entire mailing list, which could cause you to lose a major portion of your subscribers. You will also probably lose all of your past message history and performance data as well.

A Personal Recommendation

In the previous section, I provided a framework for you to evaluate and compare multiple email service providers. There are many good email service providers that will serve your email marketing efforts perfectly well. But if you have done some looking and just can't decide which email service provider is right for you, I can wholeheartedly recommend Drip (getdrip.com).

Drip is a modern platform that offers all of the functionality that you would expect from an email service provider, including list management, templating, performance tracking, mail scheduling, and marketing automation. The service is intuitive and easy to use, makes the process of adding an opt-in form to your website very easy, and the company offers great customer support. Finally, Drip offers a number of helpful tutorial videos that will help you learn their software quickly.

There are only two minor downsides to be aware of with Drip. First, many major opt-in form plugins and services do not yet integrate with Drip. While Drip does offer multiple types of opt-in forms that you can add to your website, they are not as customizable or feature-rich as other dedicated plugins. Second, Drip does not have a free tier for low-usage users and is a bit pricier than MailChimp and some other competitors at lower tiers. However, Drip is still a fantastic service that will serve every email marketer well.

Please note that I do not receive any affiliate commissions or any other form of compensation for endorsing Drip.

Email Service Provider Costs

The ongoing monthly cost of using an email service provider will be based primarily on the size of your mailing list and the frequency that you email your list. When you are first getting started, several email service providers offer a free tier that allow you to build a mailing list of a few thousand subscribers before you have to start paying an ongoing monthly fee.

For example, Mailchimp allows you to build a list of 2,000 subscribers on their free tier. As your list grows to 10,000 subscribers, you can expect to pay $50.00-$75.00 per month with most providers.

Your monthly fee will continue to grow as your list grows, but do not let that be a major concern. Paying a large monthly email service provider is simply the cost of success. I am currently paying about $2,000 per month to SendGrid for a package that allows me to send 10 million emails monthly. While the monthly fee is a big number, it is a small price to pay given that email marketing generates more than $1 million per year in revenue for my company.

Wrap-Up

Your email service provider will become the foundation of all of your email marketing efforts. They will provide the software and network infrastructure needed, so you do not have to focus on the technical intricacies of sending out email at scale. With a high-quality ESP in place, you can focus on growing your mailing list, writing marketing content, and generating revenue from your list.

Action Steps

- Research and compare email service providers.

- Select an email service provider and register for an account.

- Become familiar with your email service provider's software platform.

Case Study #1

MarketBeat

MarketBeat.com (formerly Analyst Ratings Network) is a digital publishing company that provides financial information to investors at all levels that I founded in January 2011. Prior to that, I had been running a financial news website called American Banking and Market News, which garnered more than one million page views per month and was generating well into five figures of advertising revenue per month.

While the business was doing well, it was very dependent upon referral traffic from Google. They sent traffic to our website, and we sent traffic back to their advertisers through Google's AdSense program. This is a great strategy as long as Google continues to send traffic, but as every entrepreneur that uses SEO has learned in the last five years, that's not always a guarantee. I wanted my business to stick around for the long term, and in order to do this, I knew we would need to cultivate a loyal audience and sell them products and services the company produces.

At the time, I wasn't quite sure what kind of product or service the company would sell, but I knew that we would need to communicate with our audience in some way other than hoping they would come back to the website at some point. It quickly became apparent to me that we needed to grow an email list. We added a popup opt-in form, an opt-in form below every article on our website, and started publishing a daily financial newsletter that contains a wrap-up of the latest stock recommendations from equities research analysts.

MarketBeat's daily newsletter ended up getting quite a bit of traction. It turns out investors tend to get emotionally invested in the stocks they own and want to hear the latest news and financial data about them. The company was able to take those tidbits of information and make them available to investors in a convenient and real-time format.

After running our newsletter for six months, we had attracted about 10,000 subscribers. At the same time, we were receiving a number of requests to add additional features and data to our newsletter. We then took that feedback and made a premium version of the daily newsletter called MarketBeat Daily Premium.

For $15.97 per month or $159.00 per year, subscribers could get their newsletter delivered earlier in the day, receive SMS or email alerts for their stocks, customize the look and feel of their newsletter, and set up a watch list to get more information about the companies they have invested in.

Our free daily newsletter continues to serve as the core communication point between the company and our subscribers. It is the only lead magnet that our company uses and serves as an effective tool to keep our subscriber base engaged with the content that we produce.

MarketBeat's subscribers love the up-to-the-minute financial news and information that are included in our newsletter. In addition to keeping our users engaged, we also use our daily newsletter as a way to share news and announcements from our company. It even helps generate revenue through cost-per-click (CPC) ads.

We launched a web-based investment research tool in 2012 called RatingsDB that is available for $19.97 per month or $199.00 per year. RatingsDB allows investors to access our full database of more than 250,000 stock recommendations and provides performance recommendations for individual brokers and analysts. By adding a second product to our lineup, we were able to get one-third of our paid subscribers to sign up for a second recurring monthly subscription.

We also recently launched a product called the All-Access Pass, which combines MarketBeat Daily Premium and RatingsDB—along with a few other features—for $34.97 per month.

Furthermore, we have been able to dramatically improve MarketBeat's opt-in rates over the years by continually split-testing our opt-in forms. We attract more than 20,000 organic opt-ins each month through our popup opt-in form, our sidebar opt-in form, and an opt-in form below each post on our website. We use a lightweight and simple form that automatically identifies typos and has a single call-to-action.

The biggest win in the last couple of years was to customize our popup on a per page basis to reference the name of the company discussed in the article. You can view MarketBeat's current popup opt-in form by navigating within your web browser to MarketBeat.com.

MarketBeat utilizes a number of email marketing automation techniques. The company has a 60-day autoresponder series that every new subscriber receives. We also send specific campaigns to subscribers based on the products and services they have or have not purchased.

For our paid products, we send out an engagement campaign to new customers that shows them how to use the product they purchased. For subscribers that haven't opened a message in six months, we send a campaign to try and get them re-engaged with our mailing list.

We utilize cart abandonment, which sends email discounts to customers that have previously purchased our services but have since cancelled. These specific campaigns have been incredibly effective at generating more sales and increasing the lifetime value of each customer.

MarketBeat generates revenue in a number of different ways, including display advertising, co-registration advertising, recurring monthly subscription products, newsletter advertising, and email list rentals.

More information about MarketBeat's revenue streams is included in the monetization chapter of this book. As of October 2015, more than 250,000 investors subscribe to MarketBeat's daily newsletter, and we send more than 10 million permission-based emails each month. Between MarketBeat.com and its sister websites, we generate more than 3.5 million page views on a monthly basis. In 2014 MarketBeat accrued $1.56 million in revenue and is on track to generate $2.5 million in revenue in 2015.

Chapter Two

Building Your Mailing List Through Your Website

If your organization is going to develop a successful email marketing campaign, you are going to need a consistent strategy to build and grow your email list. One of the foundational elements of every list-building initiative should be collecting email sign-ups on your website. People who are interested in your business or nonprofit are probably already visiting your website on a weekly or monthly basis. It makes a lot of sense, therefore, to use your website as one of your primary means of gathering email sign-ups.

Lead Magnets

You should offer your subscribers something of value in exchange for signing up for your email list, such as a discount coupon, a free report, or a resource list. In the world of email marketing, this is known as a lead magnet. Many website visitors are hesitant to enter their email address into an opt-in form on a website because of the perceived risk of receiving more unwanted spam email. You need to develop a compelling and valuable offer so that your potential subscribers will desire your lead magnet enough to outweigh any potential fear of receiving more unwanted email. Your subscribers know that their email address is valuable to you, and you need to offer them something of equal value in return.

A good lead magnet will help your website visitors learn a specific skill, solve a specific problem, or accomplish a specific task. The lead magnet on any given page of your website should be directly related to the content on that page. This may require creating multiple lead magnets for different parts of your website over time, but the additional work will significantly improve your opt-in rates.

Types of Lead Magnets

Here are a few common varieties of lead magnets that are typically offered in opt-in forms:

- **Free Report or Guide** – Free reports are the most common type of lead magnet. It should help your users learn about something they are interested in or help them accomplish a specific goal. For example, if you had a website about marketing, you might offer a free guide that helps people create their first Facebook ad campaign. The content of your free report should not otherwise be available on your website.

- **Resource List** – A resource list is simply a list of products, services, tools, and worksheets that will help your subscribers get started more quickly with what you want to teach them. If you had a personal finance blog, you might offer your subscribers a list of software budgeting tools and worksheets to keep track of their debt, ensure they have the right kinds of insurance, and determine whether they are saving enough for retirement.

- **Free Trial** – If you run a software-as-a-service (SaaS) company, you might consider offering a 30-day trial of your service as a lead magnet. Offering a free trial will get users engaged in your SaaS application and give you the opportunity to send them marketing content via email.

- **Educational Videos** – If you are good in front of a camera, you might record a series of instructional videos using your webcam. You can also record a screencast of an application, like Adobe Photoshop or Microsoft Excel, to show users how to perform a specific task like removing scratches from a photo in Photoshop or creating a pivot table in Excel.

- **Downloadable Software** – If your company or organization produces any kind of downloadable software, you might consider requiring a user to enter their email address in order to download your software.

- **Discounts or Free Shipping** – E-commerce stores often offer a one-time use coupon for 10% or 20% off a customer's first order as their lead magnet. While offering a discount might lower the total price of a customer's first order, it will significantly increase the probability that a website visitor will become a customer in the first place, because they will be receiving email about your company's products and services.

- **Catalog or Sales Material** – If your company sells business-to-business services or offers a product with a high price point, sending a product catalog or additional sales materials can serve as an effective lead magnet.

- **Physical Products** – If having a subscriber's physical mailing address is important to you, you can offer an inexpensive-to-produce physical product as your lead magnet. Small tools such as flashlights, knives, and screwdrivers are often used as physical product lead magnets. In order to make up the cost of producing and mailing a physical product, you can also charge a small shipping and handling fee that will generally pay for both the product and the shipping. Digital Marketer's SurvivalLife.com offers a "free" credit card knife for $4.95 shipping and handling. While they likely break even on their lead magnet, they acquire the email address, phone number, and full mailing address of everyone that completes their opt-in form.

Lead Magnet Examples

At MarketBeat, we use our free daily email newsletter as our primary lead magnet. We set the expectation to our subscribers that they are going to receive emails containing up-to-the-minute financial news and stock recommendations on a daily basis. By setting this expectation in advance, users will not be surprised by the relatively large volume of emails we send out. Through this daily interaction we also have the opportunity to promote our premium products in our newsletter and insert cost-per-click (CPC) ads for advertisers. We have tested other types of lead magnets in the past, but our daily newsletter has outperformed everything else we have tested.

At USGolfTV, we use web-based training videos as our lead magnets. A website visitor might opt in to receive a series of five videos about how to improve their putting or how to fix their slice. They have to verify their email address to receive the first video and will receive an additional video each day for the following four days. After the video series is complete, the subscriber will begin to receive our weekly email newsletter and marketing content for USGolfTV's premium video training courses. The content in our lead magnets is often closely related to our premium video products, which makes for a smooth transition between sending our free video content and promoting our paid products.

Filly Flair (fillyflair.com) and Chelsea's Boutique (chelseasboutiqueonline.com) use discounts as their primary lead magnets. These two online clothing boutiques have recognized that their customers love getting a good deal and have leveraged that reality in their lead magnets. Chelsea's Boutique offers a generous discount of 20% off to each new subscriber's next purchase. Filly Flair offers a coupon that provides a $5.00 discount regardless of order size. By offering a coupon to new subscribers, these boutiques are increasing the likelihood that a customer will place another order quickly because they want to make use of their coupon.

More Lead Magnet Ideas

If you are not sure what lead magnet will work best for your website, there are a large number of resources available online that offer specific ideas for lead magnets. A Google search for "lead magnet ideas" will return dozens of pages of articles that contain lead magnets you can model. You can also check out the websites of some of your competitors to see what kinds of lead magnets they are offering and get some more industry-specific ideas.

Do not agonize over the task of creating a lead magnet. It does not necessarily need to be long, complicated, or take a lot of work to create. You may be able to repurpose a piece of content that you have already created as your lead magnet, or even use a piece of content that someone else has made. For example, I once used a free guide produced by the Financial Industry Regulatory Authority (FINRA). Your lead magnet can be as simple as a one-page report or a list of your favorite tools and resources.

Regardless of what you choose as your lead magnet, remember that it should be a piece of content valuable to your readers. It should be closely related to the content on your website and should teach your readers how to accomplish a specific task, learn a specific skill, or solve a specific problem.

Messaging and Copy

After you have created your lead magnet, you will need to identify what kind of messaging you are going to use to get your potential subscribers to sign up for your mailing list. The language that you use on your opt-in forms will have a dramatic impact on the number of email sign-ups you receive. By creating a compelling and relevant offer, and using strong language with clear calls-to-action, you will get much higher opt-in rates.

Before looking at opt-in form software, you will first need to write the actual text (or copy) that will appear on your opt-in form. You will need to write a short headline, which will be the first piece of text that a potential subscriber reads. Then you need a description that provides more detail about what the user can expect to receive when they give you their email address. You will also need to decide what kind of information to collect on your form and what you want on the text of your clickable button.

Writing Your Headline

The headline on your opt-in form is the first piece of copy that your potential subscribers will see, and may be the most important words that you write in your business. A good headline will create desire for your lead magnet and encourage potential subscribers to read your opt-in description.

In contrast, a bad headline will be quickly passed over and ignored. It should be short, engaging, and briefly communicate what your website visitors will receive if they sign up for your mailing list.

Typically, the best headlines are between five and ten words in length and will ideally fit into a single line of text.

Here are some examples of headlines I have personally used:

- Receive Analysts' Upgrades and Downgrades Daily

- [Company Name] – Receive News and Ratings Daily

- Frustrated with Your Putting Skills?

- Learn to Eliminate the "Blow-Up Hole" (free video!)

- Add 20+ Yards to Your Drives Today!

Writing Your Description

The description on your opt-in form is the main copy that explains your lead magnet, sets the expectation for the type of email your recipients will receive, and provides an overall value proposition for why someone might want to be on your mailing list.

Your description should be between 20 and 50 words in length, and it should be clear and concise. Avoid unnecessary words, and keep your description as short as possible while fully explaining your value proposition and setting a high expectation for the emails they will receive. Finally, include a call-to-action which instructs readers to complete the opt-in form.

Here is the current opt-in description we are using on MarketBeat.com:

> Enter your email address below to receive a concise daily summary of analysts' upgrades, downgrades, and new coverage with MarketBeat.com's FREE daily email newsletter.

Selecting Your Button Text

The text on your sign-up button will be the shortest part of your opt-in that you write. Your button text may only be two or three words, but having the right text on your sign-up button can improve your opt-in rates by 10-30%. Most websites use a very generic button text like "Submit," "Get Instant Access," or "Subscribe Now." Because web users are used to clicking on buttons that say "Subscribe" and "Submit," using a generic button text will work reasonably well. I am currently using "Sign-Up Now (Free)" as the text on my buttons, which has outperformed more than a dozen other variations I have tried.

You can also try creating a unique button text that ties into the copy in your title and description. At Microconf 2015, a conference for software entrepreneurs, copywriter Joanna Wiebe shared how she tested changing the button text on one of Dressipi.com's landing pages.

Dressipi is a service that helps women find clothes that look nice and fit well, regardless of a woman's shape or size. She changed their button text from "Sign Up Now" to "Show Me Outfits I'll Love" and saw an increase of 123.9% in the rate that the button was clicked.[15] By tying Dressipi's button text into the copy of the rest of the opt-in form, she immediately saw higher opt-in rates.

Types of Opt-In Forms

Opt-in forms come in many different shapes and sizes and can be put on many different places in your website's layout. Some are small and less intrusive, such as in a sidebar or below the fold of a website, but are less likely to be seen by users. Others are larger, well-placed, and hard to miss, and will generally get much better opt-in rates. As the use of opt-in forms on websites has expanded in the last decade, several broad categories of opt-in forms have been created by the Internet marketing community.

Here are some common types of opt-in forms that are used on the web today:

- **Entry Popup** – This is a rectangular opt-in form that appears at the center of the user's screen when they first navigate to your website. Typically, the rest of the web page will be dimmed to place an emphasis on the opt-in form. Entry popups will also usually contain an "X" or "close" button that allows users to exit the opt-in form so they can view the rest of the website. To avoid being overly intrusive, many webmasters will only show a popup to their users the first time they visit their website each week. Entry popups are an extremely effective tool to gather email opt-ins and often have rates three to five times higher than an opt-in form in a sidebar or at the bottom of an article. You can view an example of an entry popup opt-in form on the MarketBeat website at MarketBeat.com.

- **Exit Popup** – An exit popup operates very similar to an entry popup, but only appears when the user has taken an action indicating they are getting ready to leave a website. If a user's mouse cursor leaves the main window of your website or if a user clicks on a link, an exit popup will appear. Webmasters sometimes choose exit popups over entry popups because they are perceived as less obtrusive, but they are also less visible than entry popups because not all users leaving a website will see an exit popup before moving on to another website.

* **Welcome Page** – A welcome page is an entry popup on steroids. A welcome page will cover the user's entire screen with a large opt-in form and require them to click a close button or scroll down to see the webpage that they are trying to access. You can view an example of a welcome page on Spencer Hawes' website, NichePursuits.com.

* **Footer Opt-In** – A footer opt-in is simply an opt-in form that appears at the bottom of an article. After a user is done reading an article on your website, they are naturally ready to read another article or take another action, such as signing up for your mailing list. Footer opt-in forms can attract highly engaged subscribers, because every subscriber that completes a footer opt-in has probably already read at least one article on your website. Footer opt-ins are also very unobtrusive, because they appear below the fold and only command a user's attention after they are reading an article. You can view an example of a footer opt-in by reading any article located on AmericanBankingNews.com.

* **Sidebar Opt-in** – A sidebar opt-in is simply an opt-in form that appears in the sidebar of your website. These often get lower opt-in rates than other types because they are not in the main column of content that a user is reading. This doesn't mean that you should avoid sidebar opt-ins altogether, because sidebar opt-ins can complement other forms on your

website. You can view an example of a sidebar opt-in by visiting AmericanBankingNews.com.

- **Hello Bar** – A hello bar is a wide, rectangular opt-in form that sits at the top or bottom of your web browser. A hello bar will typically be about 50 pixels tall and span the entire width of your screen. Because of their relatively small size, a hello bar will typically only have a headline, a textbox for your email address, and a submit button. You can see what a hello bar might look like on your website by using the demo tool provided on HelloBar.com.

- **Scroll Box** – A scroll box is a square or rectangular box that appears in the bottom right corner of your website after a user scrolls down. A scroll box will float above the rest of the content on your website and is generally viewed as unobtrusive because they do not cover up the main content of your website. You can view a demo of a scroll box or add one to your website using the plugin produced by SumoMe at sumome.com/app/scroll-box.

Which Opt-In Forms Work Best?

While there are several types of opt-in forms that you can place on your website, some work much better than others. As a baseline, I recommend implementing an entry popup and a footer opt-in form on your website. The entry popup will be visible to everyone that visits your website for the first time. The footer opt-in will catch the attention of readers that have finished reading an article. If you want to be more aggressive, you can also add a sidebar opt-in form to your website in addition to the prior two suggestions.

Using multiple opt-in forms on your website will generate a higher opt-in rate than using any single opt-in form because users that miss your entry popup may sign up through another opt-in form on your website.

Keep your opt-in forms simple in order to maximize their effectiveness. Use the minimum amount of copy necessary in your headline and description to ensure your potential subscribers will read all of your copy. A simple and consistent value proposition is the best route, because it lets users know exactly what they are getting in exchange for their email address. While it is tempting to try to collect a lot of information about your users up front, such as their name, gender, and interests, your best bet is to only ask for their email address on your opt-in form. Asking for additional information beyond a user's email address will make them less likely to complete your opt-in form. You can always ask for additional personal details later in your autoresponder series.

Your opt-in forms should have a good validation script to make sure users are entering valid email addresses into your form. If a user doesn't enter an email address and tries to click the submit button, they should receive an error message telling them they didn't complete the required field. If a user enters something that is not in the format of a valid email address, they should receive a different message informing them of such. If a user makes a common typo, such as indicating their email address is from "@gmial.com" or "@hotmial.com", your opt-in form should automatically warn the user that they may have typed in their email address wrong.

Ideally, your plugin will do these validation tasks for you. If you are using a form that you created yourself or one a developer made for you, you can use a script called MailCheck.js to automatically check for erroneous emails at: github.com/mailcheck/mailcheck.

While I recommend using an entry popup, a footer opt-in form, simple and clean copy, and minimal form elements, what works well for my companies may not work equally well for yours. Your website will have a different structure and audience than mine, so your mileage may vary with the recommendations listed above.

For this reason, it is important to regularly test different messaging, lead magnets, and opt-in form plugins to see if you can improve your opt-in rates. Consider the recommendations listed above to be a good baseline until you find something that works better for your website.

Worried about Annoying Your Users?

Some webmasters will refuse to place large and hard-to-miss opt-in forms like popups and welcome pages because they believe those types of opt-in forms are obtrusive, annoying, and degrade the user's overall experience. Do not let any personal feelings or opinions you might have stop you from using large opt-in forms. Remember that you are not your users.

Many technology enthusiasts think that all ads are annoying and should be avoided, but that doesn't mean that your potential subscribers think the same.

Your subscribers may be glad that you have a large opt-in form that appears when they first visit your website because they want your lead magnet and other email content that you produce.

If you truly believe that a large opt-in form or a popup is too annoying for your users, let the data do the talking. Run a split-test with half of your website visitors seeing the opt-in form and the other half not seeing the opt-in form at all. If the users who see the opt-in form visit the same average number of pages on your website that users who do not see the opt-in form do, you know the opt-in form is not driving any visitors away from your website.

Common Opt-in Form Plugins and Services

In order to design and place opt-in forms on your website, you will most likely need to make use of an opt-in form plugin or a cloud-based opt-in form service. As email marketing has grown in popularity over the years, a number of high-quality opt-in form plugins have been developed for all major content management systems. They will provide templates that allow you to customize the look-and-feel of your opt-in form and generate the HTML, CSS, and JavaScript necessary for your opt-in forms to run. These plugins will also integrate with your email service provider (ESP), so new sign-ups are automatically funneled to your ESP.

Here are some of the most popular opt-in form plugins:

- **OptinMonster** – OptinMonster (optinmonster.com) is a widely-used service that can place many different types of opt-ins on your website. This service integrates with all content management systems, has integrated split-testing functionality, and enables you to use custom messaging on a per page or per category basis. OptinMonster works with nearly all email service providers including MailChimp, AWeber, Infusionsoft, Constant Contact, and 15 others. While OptinMonster is incredibly flexible and feature-rich, it is one of the few services that charge an ongoing monthly fee for its use. If you receive more than 500 visitors per month, it may be worthwhile to pay the $9-$29 monthly fee to use their service.

- **Optin Cat** – Optin Cat (fatcatapps.com/optincat) is a WordPress plugin created by Fatcat Apps. Optin Cat allows you to add popups, sidebar widgets, post boxes (forms that can be placed at the bottom of a post or inside any post or page), and 2-step opt-in forms to your website. Optin Cat's popups have extremely customizable targeting options (based on time on page, number of pageviews, scrolled down percentage, category, exit intent, etc.). Optin Cat also allows you to customize the content of your messages on a per-category basis. The plugin is available for a one-time fee of $59.00.

- **SumoMe List Builder** – SumoMe (sumome.com) offers a highly customizable list-building script called List Builder that can be added to any website. List Builder works either as an entry popup or exit popup and works with most major email service providers. SumoMe is a freemium service that allows you to use their basic tools for free, but more advanced features, such as split-testing, cost as much as $99.00 per month.

- **HelloBar** – HelloBar (hellobar.com) is a service that allows you to integrate a hello bar, entry popup, scroll box, or welcome page on your website. The look and feel of their forms are highly customizable and are mobile friendly. HelloBar is currently a free service, but it doesn't integrate with any email service providers.

- **Optin Revolution** – Optin Revolution (optinrevolution.com) is a WordPress plugin that will create entry and exit popups on your website. It works with all major email service providers and has integrated split testing tools. It differentiates itself from other popup plugins by allowing users to integrate video and other rich media directly into your opt-in forms. Option Revolution Pro is available for a one-time fee of $77.00.

- **Popup Domination** – Popup Domination (popupdomination.com) is a WordPress plugin that will allow you to create entry and exit popups on your website. It features integrated A/B testing and analytics and allows you to show different popups on a per-page or per-category basis. Popup Domination offers very visually appealing opt-in form templates that are a step above many other opt-in form plugins. Popup Domination works with all major email service providers and is available for a one-time fee of $47.00.

- **Bloom** – Bloom (elegantthemes.com/plugins/bloom/) is a newer WordPress opt-in plugin created by Elegant Themes. Bloom can add an entry popup, footer opt-in form, or sidebar opt-in form to your website. It boasts more than 100 customizable templates, has integrated A/B testing, and works with nearly all major email service providers. Bloom is available as part of Elegant Themes' membership program, which costs $89.00 per year.

Which Opt-In Plugin Is Best?

There are dozens of different opt-in form plugins that you can choose from. While it would be nice to recommend an opt-in form plugin that is ideally suited to everyone, there's just no one-size-fits-all plugin that works for everyone in every situation. Some opt-in form plugins and services are specific to a single content management system, such as WordPress or Drupal. Other opt-in plugins only create certain types of opt-in forms, such as landing pages, exit popups, or entry popups.

I recommend looking at the marketing material for all of the opt-in plugins previously listed and find one that meets your specific needs. If your website runs WordPress, you will have a number of different opt-in form plugins to choose from. If your website is powered by another platform, you can use a cloud-based opt-in form service such as SumoMe, OptinMonster, or HelloBar.

Special Considerations for Opt-in Forms

You should make sure that the opt-in form you select doesn't negatively impact the load speed of your website. Some opt-in plugins are written much more efficiently than others. If your opt-in plugin noticeably slows down how fast your website loads, you should probably switch to a different plugin or service.

You can test the impact of your opt-in form plugin on your website's load speed using a tool called GTMetrix (gtmetrix.com). Test your website first before installing your opt-in form, and test it again after putting your opt-in form in place. If the addition of your opt-in software slows down your website's load speed by more than a second, it probably wasn't written very efficiently.

In special situations, it may be better to have a custom opt-in form created by a front-end web developer. I personally do not use any third-party opt-in plugins on my websites. A while back, I hired a developer to create a lightweight, custom opt-in form on my website that would work as an entry popup, a footer opt-in form, and a sidebar opt-in form. By having a custom script written, I was able to reduce the file size of the opt-in script from about 150K to about 12KB. This significantly improved my website's load speed. I was also able to integrate better form validation through MailCheck.js than was available with the off-the-shelf plugin I was using previously. However, it will not make sense for you to have a custom opt-in script created by a web developer when you are first getting started because you need a simpler option.

Many large websites still use off-the-shelf opt-in plugins. However, if you have a very popular website, need some custom functionality added to your opt-in form, or are very concerned about the load speed of your website, it may then make sense to use a custom opt-in form created by a web developer.

How Many Opt-Ins Can I Expect?

Asking how many opt-ins you should expect to receive on your website is one of the most common questions I hear from new email marketers. The volume of opt-ins that you can expect will be totally dependent on how much traffic your website receives, the quality of that traffic, and the effectiveness of your opt-in forms.

If you are getting 20,000 page views per month on your website, you are probably going to receive twice as many opt-ins than you would if you only had 10,000 page views per month. If most of your visitors come to your website from search engines and other websites similar to yours, you are likely going to get better opt-in rates, because people doing searches and looking at websites similar to yours are either doing research or are generally more engaged than people that wander onto your website from social media or unrelated websites. Working to attract a steadily growing stream of high-quality traffic is the single best way to set yourself up to build a large mailing list.

The size, number, design, content, and placement of your opt-in forms will have a dramatic impact on your opt-in rate. When you are first getting started with email marketing, you will not have any idea what combination of lead magnets, messaging, and opt-in forms will yield the highest opt-in rates.

Your best bet is to start with the practices I have outlined earlier in this chapter, and do a large number of split-tests over time to determine if there are ways that you can improve your opt-in rates from the baseline that I recommend.

A highly effective set of opt-in forms on a website with good traffic sources might yield an opt-in rate of 4-5%. A less effective set of opt-in forms on the same website might only command an opt-in rate of 0.5%. There is no industry standard for what opt-in rates you should expect, so do not beat yourself up if you get low rates for the first few months of your email marketing efforts. Instead, focus on whether or not your opt-in rates are *improving* every month.

Let's say that during the first month of your email marketing initiative that you get 20,000 page views and 200 opt-ins. You had an opt-in rate of 1%. During the second month, your website attracts a bit more traffic and receives 25,000 page views. You set up a highly effective popup opt-in form, and you receive 500 opt-ins. Your opt-in rate grew to 2% during the second month. During the third month, your traffic stays flat at 25,000 page views, but you identify a highly effective lead magnet and you attract 750 new opt-ins. Your opt-in rate just grew to 3%. By making a series of improvements and running a series of split-tests, your opt-in rates will slowly improve over time.

What If My Website Doesn't Get Much Traffic?

If you are just getting started and your website is not getting much traffic yet, you should still place opt-in forms on your website. It takes time to create a popular website and build a large mailing list. You may only get 50 or 100 opt-ins per month for the first several months of operating your website, and that's okay. Your total list size will continue to grow as weeks and months go on. As new subscribers sign up , your list will grow in size like a snowball rolling down a hill. Before you know it, you will have a few thousand people on your mailing list that want to receive email from you on a regular basis.

While growing the amount of traffic your website receives is beyond the scope of this book, there are a number of great resources available that can teach you how to build a popular website. The book *Traction* by Gabriel Weinberg provides an overview of 19 different marketing channels you can use to grow your business and get more people onto your website. There are a number of books in the "For Dummies" series that teach traffic generation concepts, such as search engine optimization, social media marketing, and Facebook marketing. DigitalMarketer.com produces a number of resources that show you how to attract more web traffic. If you are not sure what marketing channels you should pursue initially, you can use SimilarWeb (similarweb.com) to see where some of your competitors are currently getting their traffic from.

Split Testing Your Opt-in Forms

The key to getting great opt-in rates is regularly running tests to determine if making changes to your forms will increase the percentage of people that complete them. In order to do this, identify one change to your forms that might improve your opt-in rates.

Show half of your website's visitors the original version of your opt-in form, and show the new variation you created to the other half. Your opt-in form software's split-testing capability will be able to handle the 50-50 split for you without having to write any code. Wait until about 300 more people complete your opt-in form.

If the two versions are equally effective, they should both receive about 150 opt-ins. If your variation gets 175 opt-ins and your original opt-in form only gets 125, you know that the change you made likely improved your opt-in rates. On the other hand, if the original opt-in form gets more opt-ins than the variation, you know that the split-test didn't work, and you should stick with your original opt-in form.

Every aspect of your opt-in forms can and should be tested. You might find that an entry popup works better than an exit popup. You might find that adding a second opt-in form to your website improves your opt-in rates. You can test changing the language in your headline, description, and button text. You can test a different lead magnet to see if it better resonates with your subscribers. You can even try changing the colors and fonts in your opt-in forms. Remember, however, that you should only test one change on your website at a time. If you make multiple changes at once, you will not know which changes are helping your opt-in rates and which are hurting them.

If your website doesn't receive a lot of opt-ins on a monthly basis, it may take a while for you to run a statistically valid split-test. If you only receive 100 opt-ins each month, it is going to take you 3-4 months to identify a clear winner. Because you can't run as many split-tests when you are first getting started, you should put significantly more thought into the changes that you evaluate. Start with big changes, such as re-writing your headline or trying a different lead magnet. Only test smaller changes like colors and button text after you have thoroughly exhausted the more visible aspects of your opt-in form.

You will eventually reach a point where your opt-in forms are honed in and you start to see diminishing returns on your split-testing efforts. This does not mean you should stop testing altogether. The effectiveness of different types of lead magnets and opt-in forms will change over time as web users' behaviors change. If you had a highly optimized set of opt-in forms three years ago and haven't done any split-testing since then, it is probably time to start testing new lead magnets, new messaging, and new types of opt-in forms.

Creating Your "Thank You" Page

The page that users are redirected to after they sign up for your mailing list is often referred to as a "thank you" page, because it usually contains a message that thanks a subscriber for signing up for a mailing list. A "thank you" page will also often contain next steps that the user should take, such as clicking a link in a confirmation email or checking out other content produced on your website. On most websites, there generally is not much content on a "thank you" page other than a brief message welcoming people to their mailing list.

Many webmasters do not realize that their thank you page is an incredibly valuable piece of ad real estate. A user that lands on your "thank you" page after opting in has already indicated they are interested in your content and have taken a specific action to receive more of it. They are much more likely than other users to take another action, such as signing up for a free trial of a premium service, clicking on a banner ad, or opting into another mailing list through a co-registration ad unit.

While you might make $10.00 in ad revenue for every 1,000 people that read an article on your website, you can make between $100.00 and $750.00 for every 1,000 new subscribers that land on your thank you page and take another action. For specific information about how to monetize your "thank you" page, read the monetization chapter of this book.

Wrap-Up

Implementing good opt-in forms on your website is your first step to building a large and profitable email list. Collecting opt-ins from your website should be the core of your list-building efforts. While other list-building strategies might require an upfront cash investment, subscribers that opt in through your website are effectively free. Spend sufficient time writing compelling copy, create a highly-desirable lead magnet, and implement an opt-in form plugin, and your mailing list will grow steadily over time.

Action Steps

- Develop a lead magnet to offer to new subscribers.

- Write the messaging (copy) that you want to use on your opt-in forms.

- Pick which opt-in form plugin or service you want to use on your website.

- Set up your opt-in form plugin and connect it to your email service provider (ESP).

- Place your opt-in forms on your website and verify that they are working.

- Set up a split-test to try to improve your opt-in rates.

Case Study #2

Bidsketch

Bidsketch (bidsketch.com) is a software-as-a-service (SaaS) company that helps freelancers and other client service businesses create proposals for their clients. The company's value proposition is that their service can help businesses create better proposals in less time. The service comes with a number of proposal templates their customers can use and also allows clients to accept proposals using electronic signatures. Bidsketch's home page boasts that its clients have earned more than $250 million using proposals generated by its software. I had the opportunity to interview Bidsketch founder Ruben Gamez as part of this book.

Email marketing is one of the primary tools that Bidsketch uses to turn website visitors into customers. While most SaaS companies try to get users to sign up for a free trial of their service, Bidsketch focuses primarily on getting users to sign up for their mailing list. The company uses a wide variety of lead magnets on its website to attract sign-ups, including free sample proposals, marketing e-books, and other educational guides. Once a user signs up for Bidsketch's mailing list, they will receive a 30-day drip campaign focused on acquiring more clients through their proposals. The educational emails that Bidsketch sends also include calls-to-action for the company's subscription service. After a user completes the 30-day drip campaign, they will get emails promoting new blog content that helps subscribers grow their business.

Gamez said that surveying his users to get ideas for lead magnets has been an incredibly effective strategy for growing his company's mailing list. By asking users what specific issues and problems they are having related to sales and marketing, and creating lead magnets that address those issues, Gamez has been able to significantly increase the number of opt-ins his company receives each month. "We do this by surveying people and having them vote on different lead magnets," Gamez said. He added, "Formstack works great for larger surveys, and Qualaroo is what we use to do micro-surveys with visitors on our website."

Jobs-to-be-done (JTBD) interviews are another strategy that Gamez has used to identify ways to grow his company's mailing list and his business. JTBD interviews help a business understand its customers' needs, motivations, and the specifics concerning the tasks they are trying to complete. He said JTBD interviews "focus on a single story, where customers gave up using a tool, found out about our product, and eventually decided to switch." He added, "You'd be amazed how many great list-building ideas you can get from the discovery part of those interviews." By learning what problems customers have with other services, how they found out about Bidsketch, and what they are trying to accomplish, Bidsketch has been able to get more opt-ins and improve the quality of service that its customers receive.

Gamez said using a "yes or no" question on an opt-in form that asks the user whether or not they want a free trial of their service has worked surprisingly well on some parts of their website. If a user answers yes to that question, they will receive a second email that pitches them Bidsketch's service and tells them how to sign up.

Bidsketch uses Drip (getdrip.com) as its email service provider. Gamez commented that Drip has "been a huge help for setting up multiple lead magnets and experimenting with all sorts of interesting workflows." He has also used Drip to test multiple autoresponder series and to streamline subscription management. In a blog post on Drip's blog, Gamez credits Drip to increasing the number of trials that his service receives by 30%.[16]

Bidsketch currently has 80,000 email subscribers and is attracting about 9,000 new email subscribers each month as of August 2015. Gamez says that he can attribute a third of the company's customers directly to email marketing. He closed by saying, "While it's tough to track with analytics, I've seen the impact of not having email in our funnel, and it's not pretty. Email marketing is one of the most important parts of our marketing strategy."

Chapter Three

14 Ways to Grow Your Mailing List Independently of Your Website

Building your mailing list through your website will allow you to steadily collect opt-ins and grow your list over time. If you want to accelerate how fast your list is growing, you can make use of some of these alternative strategies that work independently of the traffic your website normally receives.

While sign-ups through your website will happen automatically once plugins are set up, the strategies listed below will require either a financial investment or a steady investment of your time and energy. Do not let this scare you off. Paid acquisition strategies can be some of the most consistent and profitable ways of making money through email marketing. For example, let's say that you can make $5.00 from each email sign-up on your mailing list and could pay $2.00 to get someone to sign up for your mailing list. You would buy as many of those leads as are available because it is better than any other investment you can possibly make. If you put $2.00 in the stock market, you will be lucky if you get a 10% return on that investment in one year, and it turns into $2.20. If you pay $2.00 to acquire an email address and can make $5.00 off it over the course of the following year, that's a return on investment of 150%. If you have a well-honed conversion funnel, spending money to acquire email sign-ups can be one of the most profitable investments you can make.

Try Co-Registration Advertising

Co-registration advertising networks allow you to advertise on other websites' "thank you" pages. After someone signs up for a mailing list on a website that is running a co-registration ad unit, they will be presented a list of offers from third-party advertisers (like you). If the subscriber selects your offer and presses the submit button, the advertising network will provide you the subscriber's contact information to add to your mailing list through an API call or by periodically sending you a spreadsheet of new sign-ups. You can expect to pay $1.00-$4.00 per sign-up through a co-registration ad network.

You can see an example of a co-registration ad unit below:

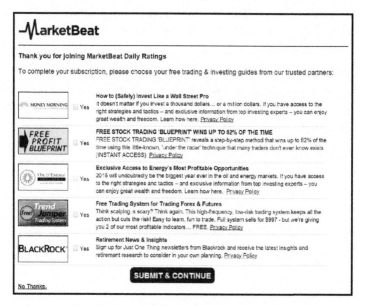

The quality of the sign-ups that you receive from co-registration advertising will vary depending on the sites that your ad is running on. When working with a co-registration ad network, I recommend asking for a list of sites that they have available for you to advertise on. Only agree to place your ads on websites that are similar to yours or are in the same industry. Subscribers that come from unrelated websites are less likely to be engaged with your content and will be less likely to purchase anything from you.

The quality of leads can also vary among multiple sites in the same industry. One site may send subscribers that connect well with your content, and another may send subscribers that are not engaged with your content and are of no value to you.

Given the ongoing cost of running a co-registration advertising campaign and the disparity of lead quality on a site-to-site basis, you will want to monitor performance on a per-ad-network and per-website basis every month. Are the subscribers that came from a particular website's co-registration ad unit as engaged as users that sign up through your website? Are they opening emails at the same rate as other subscribers? Are they clicking on links? Are they buying products and services from you at the same rate as other subscribers? While running a co-registration advertising campaign can be incredibly profitable, you must monitor your campaign's performance regularly to weed out underperforming websites and ad networks.

Co-registration advertising is more prominently used in some industries than others. You will frequently see these units on financial websites, sports websites, travel websites, business opportunity websites, and disaster preparation websites. While you can run a co-registration advertising campaign for a website in just about any niche, it works better for some industries than others.

Here are some of the largest co-registration advertising networks:

- **After Offers** – After Offers (afteroffers.com) works with advertisers and publishers with travel websites, financial websites, Internet business websites, and survival/disaster preparation websites.

- **CoregMedia** – CoregMedia (coregmedia.com) is a general co-registration advertising network that works with publishers and advertisers in a large number of industries. CoregMedia advertises that it works with many major advertisers like Kohl's,

Nokia, Gap, Dish Network, Red Lobster, and Wal-Mart.

* **Investing Media Solutions** – Investing Media Solutions (investingmediasolutions.com) works with advertisers and publishers with financial websites.

* **Investing Channel** – Investing Channel (investingchannel.com) also works with publishers and advertisers with financial websites.

* **Opt-Intelligence** – Opt-Intelligence (optintelligence.com) is one of the largest co-registration advertising platforms online. Opt-Intelligence works with many major advertisers and publishers in a wide variety of industries.

* **Tiburon Media** – Tiburon Media (tiburonmedia.com) is a general co-registration advertising network that works with a number of major companies including Microsoft, Adobe, Cisco, Dell, Disney, and Toyota.

Swap Email Sends with Other Mailing List Owners

If you have built up a mailing list of a few thousand subscribers, swapping email sends with other mailing list owners can be an extremely effective way to grow your mailing list. When you do an email swap, you will send a marketing email to your subscribers on behalf of another website, and they will send an email that you write to *their* mailing list.

The email that you send to your email swap partner's list should attempt to get their subscribers to sign-up for your mailing list. The email should contain some kind of offer or lead magnet and contain multiple links to a page on your website that has an opt-in form. If you do not have a page dedicated to collecting email sign-ups on your website, create one now. This is called a landing page.

Note that you should never send your actual mailing list to your email swap partner, and they should never send their actual mailing list to you. Your swap partner will send out your email to their subscribers, and you will send out your swap partner's message to yours. Your mailing list should be treated like classified information. It should never be given to any third party under any circumstances. You do not know what kind of spam an unscrupulous partner might send to your list, so it is best to keep that information under tight wraps.

In order to find email swap partners, make a list of as many websites as you can that are similar to yours. Review your list, and remove any websites that do not have opt-in forms on them. It is unlikely that a website has a mailing list if they are not actively soliciting opt-ins. If possible, try to make a list of 100 different websites that you could potentially swap email sends with. Go through your list and send an introductory email to each website's owner that provides some background information about you and your website. Tell them that you are actively seeking for other websites to do email swaps with. Ask if they have a mailing list and if they would be interested in doing a swap with your list. Since email swaps are generally a no-lose proposition for both parties, you will find that many other webmasters are more than happy to do email swaps with you.

If you want to streamline the process of finding email swap partners, you can use a service called Safe Swaps (safe-swaps.com) to locate webmasters who are interested in doing email swaps with other mailing list owners. Safe Swaps is a paid service that costs $29.95 per month to use.

Email List Rentals

If you have a sizable advertising budget to grow your mailing list, you can pay other mailing list owners to email their list on your behalf. Email list rentals work similar to email swaps. Instead of repaying the list owner by mailing your list on their behalf, you will pay them a negotiated fee for the privilege of their mailing list. Afterwards, you will create an email that contains an offer for some kind of lead magnet and a link to sign up for your mailing list. The list owner then sends the promotional email to their mailing list on a set date and time for the agreed-upon fee.

Email list rentals are typically sold on a cost per thousand (CPM) basis. If you wanted to email 10,000 subscribers on someone else's mailing list and they charged a $25.00 CPM, you would pay a $250.00 fee. Prices for email list rentals can vary dramatically depending on what industry or niche the mailing list is in. For example, emailing a list of investors will cost much more than emailing a list of computer gamers, because selling products to investors is much more profitable. For lower-end categories of mailing lists, you might be able to rent an email list for $10.00-$20.00 CPM. For high-end categories of mailing lists, you might pay $50.00-$100.00 CPM to email someone else's list.

In the Internet marketing space, you might see email list rentals referred to as "solo ads." In other spaces, you might see email list rentals referred to as "dedicated email sends." Do not let this throw you off. "Solo ads" and "dedicated email sends" are just another name for email list rentals.

There are a number of online databases that advertise email lists available for rent. NextMark (nextmark.com) is probably the largest online database of email, phone, and snail mail mailing lists with more than 60,000 mailing lists available for rental. Unfortunately their search tool is a bit antiquated, so you may have to comb through several pages of results to find a list that you want to email.

A wide range of quality exists among email list rental providers. Since you never actually see the provider's subscriber list, there is no way to independently verify the size or quality of their mailing list. While many email list rental providers are professional and completely above board, there are some unscrupulous providers that try to pass off compiled lists, purchased lists, and unrelated mailing lists as a high-quality and relevant list available for rental. Because of the level of trust involved, you should only work with very reputable mailing list owners. If possible, consider using an agency that works with advertisers in your industry to do email list rentals. A good email advertising agency will already have relationships with mailing list owners in your industry and can mitigate the possibility of working with dishonest mailing list owners.

Do Not Buy a Mailing List

While renting an email list is a commonly accepted practice in the email marketing industry, buying an email list is not advisable under any circumstances. When renting a list, you are paying a list owner to email their list on your behalf. You are effectively borrowing the permission that their subscribers have given the list owner to email them. While there is nothing that's necessarily illegal or immoral about purchasing a mailing list, generally it's a bad idea, because individuals on a purchased list have not opted in and haven't given you permission to email them.

Using purchased email lists in order to get customers is usually not a very effective marketing strategy. Most email lists available for sale are low-quality, out-of-date, and are not maintained very well. People on these lists won't find your content engaging and won't want to receive your emails. More importantly, they are very unlikely to buy anything from you or respond to any of your offers.

Many email service providers (ESPs) will not let you use a purchased list with their services because of the damage that mailing a purchased list can do to the reputation of your domain name and IP address. Emailing purchased lists usually results in an unacceptably large number of spam complaints and undeliverable emails. This runs the risk of your domain name and IP address being added to a blacklist, which causes your future mailings to end up in subscribers' spam folders or not be delivered at all. In order to maintain your reputation, your best bet is to only email people that have directly given you permission to do so.

Make Your Email Content Shareable

If you publish an email newsletter, place social media sharing buttons and a "forward to a friend" link in each of your newsletters. These buttons will encourage your current email subscribers to share and forward your email content to their friends and other people in their social networks, giving you new connections and access to potential new subscribers. You can also consider placing a call-to-action at the bottom of your newsletter with a link to subscribe, which will encourage anyone who received a forwarded copy of your newsletter to sign up for your mailing list. Most email service providers include tools to make your email content shareable, so it shouldn't require much work to add social sharing and "forward to a friend" links to your emails.

Archive Email Content on Your Website

Whenever you publish an email newsletter or another piece of informational or educational content, post a copy of that email into an archive of newsletter content on your website. If you are using WordPress, this might mean creating a new category for newsletter content and publishing any new newsletter content as a post in that category. Whenever you add a new email newsletter to the archive, share it on all of your available social media channels. This will broaden the reach of your email content and make it visible to followers not already on your email list. It will also provide a second way for your subscribers to see your new content if they happen to miss your email. Google and other search engines will also index the archive of newsletter content on your website, which may also increase the quantity of organic search traffic that you receive.

Own a Physical Store?

If you own a physical store or have any other kind of retail location, ask every customer if they want to sign up for your email list at checkout. You can ask each customer something like, "Would you like to sign up for our mailing list and periodically get coupons in your email?" If the customer says yes, have them write down their email address on a sign-up sheet on a clipboard. At the end of the day, add these customers to your mailing list.

Leverage Your Email Signature

Adjust your and your employees' email signatures so they contain a call-to-action and a link to sign up for your mailing list.

Here's a simple email signature with a call-to-action that I have used in the past:

Run a Contest or Giveaway

Find something of high-perceived value that you can use as a giveaway or a contest prize, like an iPad or an iPhone. Require everyone participating in the contest to sign up for your mailing list in order to enter the contest. Promote the contest through your personal and company social media channels, as well as any other marketing channels you might have available. Remember to add social sharing buttons to the contest page on your website, so it is easily shareable.

Social Media Offers

Develop a high-value lead magnet or another offer, such as an ebook or free report, and share it on all of your available social media channels. Require that users enter their email address in order to access the lead magnet or other offered item.

Make sure you use every social media channel you have available, including Facebook, Twitter, LinkedIn, Instagram, Pinterest, Tumblr, and other social media profiles that you have set up. Share the offer through both your personal social media accounts and any profiles for your business. Share the offer multiple times over the course of a few weeks for maximum exposure.

YouTube Annotations and Links

If you or your company have a YouTube channel, add calls-to-action and hyperlinks in your videos to subscribe to your mailing list. Include hyperlinks in annotations and your video description that direct viewers to a landing page on your website where users can opt in to your mailing list or respond to another offer.

To learn how to create annotations in your YouTube videos, HubSpot has put together a quick guide that demonstrates this process:

- blog.hubspot.com/marketing/how-to-annotate-youtube-video.

Set Up Google AdWords

If you have money to invest in your list-building campaign, you can use Google AdWords to drive traffic to a landing page, where users can enter their email address in exchange for a lead magnet or another offer. Make sure you use the conversion tracking pixel that Google provides in order to identify which keywords and ads are driving the most opt-ins.

After your campaign has been running a while, you can use Google's cost-per-action (CPA) bidding to optimize for email sign-ups. AdWords also has an extension that allows advertisers to place an opt-in form directly in search results, but that feature is currently only available to a select group of publishers. While creating a Google AdWords campaign is beyond the scope of this book, I recommend reading *Ultimate Guide to Google AdWords* by Perry Marshall and Mike Rhodes if you want to learn how to create a Google AdWords campaign.

Presenting at a Trade Show?

If your organization is presenting at a trade show, you have a prime opportunity to gather new email sign-ups. Run a giveaway and offer a highly desirable prize. New electronic gadgets such as iPads, Kindles, and video game systems work great as prizes. Allow attendees to enter your drawing by dropping their business card into a fishbowl. You will need to make it clear that contest participants are signing up for your mailing list.

At the end of the conference, pick a winner and then add all participants to your mailing list. Send a welcome email to every new mailing list member. Your welcome email should remind them about the contest, why they have been added to your mailing list, and provide information about your products and services. You should also include an opt-out link in your welcome email so that anyone who doesn't want to receive email from you can easily unsubscribe.

Put QR Codes in Your Print Marketing Material

If your business makes use of print marketing material, add a QR code that users can easily scan with their phones. Use the code to redirect users to a mobile-friendly landing page on your website where you can ask them to opt in to your mailing list. You can easily create a QR code using any number of websites that offer free generators, such as qr-code-generator.com. Also include a short URL that redirects to your mobile-friendly landing page directly below the QR code. Not everyone has a QR code scanner on their phone, and it may be easier for them to simply type a URL into their smartphone's web browser or write it down for later use.

Add a Facebook Page Call-To-Action

If your organization has a Facebook business page set up, you can add a call-to-action button on the header of your Facebook page to attract email sign-ups. In order to create a call-to-action button on your organization's Facebook page, navigate to your page, and click the "Create Call to Action" button in the header of your page. You can choose between a number of button texts including "book now," "contact us," "use app," "play game," "shop now," "sign up," and "watch video." I personally recommend using "sign up" because it's simple and it tends to convert well. You will also be asked to provide the URL where users can then add themselves to your mailing list. The URL should be a landing page that provides an introduction to your mailing list and a form so users can easily sign up.

How to Create a Landing Page to Collect Opt-Ins

Throughout this chapter, there are several strategies that discuss sending traffic to a landing page to collect email addresses. A landing page is a single purpose webpage that exists solely to persuade users to take a specific action, such as completing an opt-in form or purchasing a product. While the process of building a landing page is beyond the scope of this book, I do want to provide a couple of basic tips and point you to some resources that can help you create landing pages for your business.

Don't try to create a landing page using raw HTML or have a landing page created by a professional designer. There are several great tools available including LeadPages (leadpages.com), Unbounce (unbounce.com), and InstaPage (instapage.com) that make creating landing pages simple. Most of them have drag-and-drop interfaces which allow you to put a great landing page together in a short amount of time. These services will also integrate with your email service provider (ESP) so your sign-up form works without any coding on your part.

Remember that the only thing on your landing page should be your opt-in form. That means no sidebars, navigation, or any other extraneous content. It should have a title, a bit of sales and marketing content, maybe a video, and your actual opt-in form. Always keep the focus on the single action you want your subscribers to take. When you add additional content to your landing pages, users are more likely to be distracted and are less likely to take the indicated action.

For more tips and recommendations about how to put a landing page together, Unbounce has compiled a resource titled "101 Landing Page Optimization Tips"[17], which provides detailed instructions on how to create landing pages that work.

The Importance of Continually Growing Your List

Even if you have a large mailing list with tens of thousands of subscribers, you should continuously work on growing your email list. A small percentage of your users will unsubscribe from your mailing list every month because they lose interest in the topic area you write about or they simply no longer want to receive your emails. There will also be some subscribers whose email addresses are no longer valid, because they switched ISPs or moved to a new email address.

You will need to continually attract new subscribers to your mailing list to replace those that drop off over time. Additionally, users tend to be most engaged with the content of a mailing list when they first subscribe. Over time, their open rates and engagement rates will naturally decline. Keep gathering new subscribers to ensure there is always a percentage of your subscribers that are highly engaged with your content.

Wrap-Up

While the bulk of your email opt-ins will likely come from your website, there are many other ways to grow your mailing list independently of your website. Not every strategy listed in this chapter will be appropriate for every organization, so take time to consider which of the 14 strategies presented in this chapter you can use to grow *your* mailing list.

Whether you want to leverage social media, do paid advertising campaigns, or run a contest, there are always more ways to accelerate your list growth beyond getting opt-ins on your website.

Action Steps

- Make a list of 100 potential partners that you can do email swaps with.

- Leverage your social media profiles to build your mailing list and promote your existing email content.

- Determine whether paid list-building strategies, including co-registration advertising, Google AdWords, and email list rentals, are appropriate for your mailing list.

- Add social sharing and "forward to a friend" buttons to your email content.

- Make a shareable archive of past email content on your website.

- Consider what other ways you can grow your list independently of opt-ins from your website.

Case Study #3

GMB Fitness

GMB Fitness (gmb.io), founded by Andy Fossett, is a website that offers home-based training programs that combine gymnastic and martial arts exercise movements for fitness enthusiasts at all levels of strength and experience. I had the opportunity to interview Fossett as part of this book. The company began by offering DVDs, but quickly transitioned to offering video training courses and membership programs. Their content teaches what they call "physical autonomy" and is delivered through a variety of exercise tutorials and online coaching.

GMB Fitness uses email as one of their primary marketing channels. Fossett said that email marketing is the single most important part of their business after the video content they produce. They have developed a variety of different opt-in forms and related autoresponder sequences based on specific goals, such as handstands and stretching. They also have a general autoresponder series that teaches their philosophy of exercise and publishes a weekly newsletter to subscribers that have completed their autoresponder series. They have also created onboarding sequences that help new customers engage with their website and the products they purchase.

Fossett told me email is also an invaluable communication tool between his company and its audience. He commented, "It gives us a chance to help them and increases their trust in us, which increases the likelihood of a beneficial long-term relationship. We also get feedback and intelligence that helps us know what our audience wants to buy and what they think of our current products. We can use that to improve our programs and marketing."

In order to attract opt-ins to their website, GMB Fitness uses a variety of mini-programs that teach about specific fitness topics their audience is interested in. Their free subscribers receive access to a "members area" that contains about a dozen free video resources that are tightly coupled with their paid products.

Fossett informed me that the most effective opt-ins scratch a specific itch. For example, their customers couldn't care less about content that teaches them how to stretch properly. However, if they package stretching instruction videos around an ailment that stretching solves, such as painful mobility, readers will sign up for those opt-ins in much greater numbers.

As GMB Fitness has gained a reputation for producing really great content, they have had the opportunity to publish guest posts on major fitness sites, which have generated a lot of opt-ins. Fossett said, "We had a series of five posts on artofmanliness.com that drove a couple thousand subscribers. We've since had a couple of large websites feature us for a series on a tight theme, and each has performed really well."

When I asked Fossett why he thinks his business does so well, he said there are no secrets. If anything, the only secret is to "work your butt off making great content for several years." Fossett and his team have worked hard to build a professional, graphically appealing website that contains great content. He commented, "We make it very clear that we are experts with quality materials, so the other stuff works easily. Without the foundation, all the best tactics can fail."

One piece of advice Fossett has to offer is: pay attention to what your messages look like on mobile devices. A study from Movable Ink finds that as many as 66% of all emails opened are done on a smartphone or tablet.[18] He said, "If your emails don't look good on an iPhone, you're missing out. You need to make sure that your messages are easy to read and click on using mobile devices." He added that there are simply no excuses for sending emails that don't render correctly on mobile, because nearly all major ESPs include mobile preview tools.

Another tip that Fossett gave was to consider re-sending an email to subscribers that don't open it. He said, "A few days after you send an email, create a segment of people who did not open it. Then change the subject line, and send it to those people again. It's a simple way to get a 10+% increase in people seeing and clicking your messages."

Fossett also reiterated the importance of testing. He advised that you should test multiple subject lines, multiple from-addresses, and multiple calls-to-action to see what works best. He also suggested testing the frequency of your autoresponder series by creating two different versions of an autoresponder series with the same messages sent at different sending frequencies to see which generates the most engagement and sales.

GMB Fitness has grown a mailing list of nearly 60,000 subscribers. Fossett informed me they are adding 1,000 new subscribers each week and hope to hit 100,000 subscribers within the next year.

The most impressive part of GMB's email statistics are its engagement numbers. He says it isn't uncommon for them to have 60% of their recipients open any one email. Nearly 80% of his company's sales come from people that are on at least one of their email lists.

He closed by saying, "The main point is that email is a great tool that can generate lots of sales and subscriptions if you use it effectively. It's a tool that reaches almost 100% of the people online, and it's relatively inexpensive to use, so the ROI on learning to leverage email effectively is probably higher than any other form of promotion."

Chapter Four

Mailing Your List: How, What, and When to Send to Your Audience

As you begin to build a mailing list, you will be faced with the challenge of regularly sending educational and marketing content to your mailing list. You will need to decide how often you want to email your list, what types of email you want to send to your audience, and whether or not you want to leverage advanced strategies like marketing automation and list segmentation. You will need to create a series of welcome emails in an autoresponder series that will help new subscribers get engaged with your content. You will also need to create a schedule of mailings so subscribers that have completed your autoresponder series continue to receive email from you on a regular basis.

The First Email Your Subscribers Receive

The first email that every new subscriber will receive from your mailing list is called the welcome email. Sending a well-written welcome email to each of your subscribers is the first step in nurturing long-term subscribers that will always be happy to receive your email. This email should accomplish a number of different tasks, including thanking subscribers for joining your mailing list, setting expectations for the type and quantity of email they are going to receive, getting your subscribers to whitelist your email address, and encouraging them to take further action.

At the top of your welcome email, include a personal message that thanks the subscriber for signing up for your mailing list. If appropriate for your industry, use personal language as if you were writing to a new friend that you just met for coffee. Next, you should tell your subscribers what kind of email they are going to receive and how often they are going to receive it. This will help your subscribers set a mental expectation for what kind of emails they should expect. You should also ask your email subscribers to whitelist your email address or add you to their safe sender list so that your messages never go to their spam folder. Feel free to copy MarketBeat's whitelist instructions page located at marketbeat.com/safe-sender. Finally, you should consider what action you want your users to take next. You might want them to read a particular piece of content on your website, persuade them to check out one of your products, or ask that they recommend your mailing list to a friend of theirs. Include a hyperlink with a clear call-to-action at the bottom of your email and thank them again for joining your list.

Here is the copy for the actual welcome email currently being used by MarketBeat:

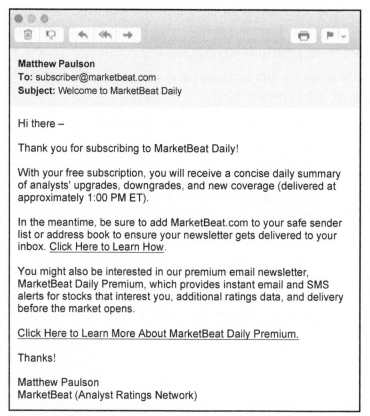

Creating an Autoresponder Series

As mentioned previously, an autoresponder series is a series of pre-written emails that every new subscriber receives in sequential order after signing up for your mailing list. A new subscriber might receive your welcome email on the first day of their subscription, another email on the third day of their subscription, another on the fifth day of their subscription, etc. The purpose of an autoresponder series is to send a consistent set of content to every new subscriber, so they can become familiar with your writing and your company's products and services.

There are six different ways that you can use the emails in your autoresponder series:

- Promoting your company's products and services

- Providing additional educational content to your subscribers

- Asking them to add your email address to their safe sender list

- Promoting another company's products as an affiliate

- Highlighting existing content on your website to your new subscribers

- Asking subscribers for feedback about your content and your company's products

Creating an autoresponder series is more of an art than a science. There is no perfect length for a series, and there is no perfect number of emails to include. You will be able to track the performance of any particular message, but it's notoriously difficult to split-test an entire autoresponder series. I recommend sending out messages anywhere from three to six days apart in your autoresponder series and having a total length between three and five months. This may mean that you are including as many as 30 emails in your autoresponder series, but it doesn't have to be a daunting task if you simply write a new email every 4-5 days as your oldest subscribers near the end of the series.

Every major email service provider (ESP) includes the ability to create a series of autoresponder messages that new subscribers will receive automatically over time on the dates that you specify. Typically, you will simply need to enter the subject line and body of your email into a form provided by your ESP.

You will also need to specify when a new subscriber will receive a particular email, such as on the 10th day of their subscription. Some email service providers will also let you push an email to the next day when an autoresponder message is scheduled to go out on a weekend or holiday when someone is unlikely to check their email.

If you want to see how an autoresponder series works in practice, consider creating a new email account and using it for the sole purpose of watching autoresponder emails come in from lists that you have signed up for. Use the single-purpose email account that you created to sign up for mailing lists of some of your competitors and well-known marketers to get ideas for your autoresponder series.

You can see all of the autoresponder emails sent out by MarketBeat or USGolfTV just by completing an opt-in form on either website. Pat Flynn (smartpassiveincome.com) also has a particularly good autoresponder series that's worth checking out.

Here's a sample layout of what an autoresponder series might look like:

- Day 1: Send your welcome email.

- Day 5: Highlight some of your website's "best-of" content.

- Day 9: Provide an introduction to your company's products and services.

- Day 13: Ask subscribers to add your email address to their safe sender list.

- Day 17: Provide a piece of educational content or training material.

- Day 21: Promote one of your company's products or services.

- Day 25: Ask subscribers for feedback about your content.

- Day 29: Promote another company's products as an affiliate.

- Day 33: Provide more educational content or training material.

- Day 37: Promote one of your company's products or services.

- Day 41: Provide links to helpful stories and resources around the web.

- Day 45: Reintroduce some older content on your website to your new subscribers.

- Day 49: Promote another company's products as an affiliate.

- Day 53: Promote one of your company's products or services.

- Day 57: Provide more educational content or training material.

- Day 61: Ask subscribers for feedback about your content again.

- Day 65: Promote one of your company's products or services.

The biggest mistake that you can make with your autoresponder series is not having one at all. If you don't regularly email your list, they will become disengaged with your content and will forget that they gave you permission to email them in the first place. If you try to email a mailing list that you haven't contacted in six months, invariably some subscribers will forget who you are and accuse you of spamming them. Sending regular emails every two to five days for the first several months of a user's subscription is arguably the best way to keep them engaged with your content and interested in your company's products and services.

Broadcast Emails

In addition to your autoresponder series, you will want to regularly send messages to your entire email list. These messages are known as broadcast emails because you are effectively broadcasting a single message to your list.

Broadcast emails are one-time messages that get sent at a specific date and time for a specific purpose. They generally don't get reused or resent again to any part of your mailing list in the future. Typically, these are sent in order to make an announcement or to get your subscribers to take a specific action, such as engaging with a piece of content or buying a specific product.

Broadcast emails serve three primary purposes. First, they keep users who have completed your autoresponder series engaged with your content. By regularly sending new educational and informational content to your mailing list, they will continue to receive value from you, will be more likely to stay engaged with your content, and will be less likely to unsubscribe. Second, sending broadcast emails is the best way to make announcements to your list and keep them informed about what's going on with your business. Finally, sending broadcast emails to promote products and services will be one of your key monetization points. You can use broadcast emails to promote your company's products and services, or you can use them to promote another company's products and services as an affiliate.

Planning Your Broadcast Email Calendar

You will want to develop a schedule of the emails that you plan to send to your mailing list in a given month prior to the first day of that month. By creating a plan ahead of time, you can space out your emails appropriately throughout the month and can create a good rhythm of educational and content emails, then sales and marketing emails. If you send too many sales emails in a row or don't take a day off from mailing your list for several days, you may upset some of your subscribers and cause them to unsubscribe from your list.

I recommend printing out a calendar from the web and physically writing down the emails that you want to send out. You don't need to write out the *entire* email you plan on sending—just the broad category of the message, such as "newsletter," "marketing email," "product launch announcement," "tip/resource," or "content promotion." By putting your broadcast email schedule on paper, you'll be able to visually see if your messages are spread out equally and aren't too focused on any single type of email.

Creating your broadcast email calendar is also more of an art than a science. There is no ideal number of emails you should send at any given month. There is no perfect frequency that suggests you should email every day, every other day, or every third day. There are no hard rules that suggest you should send at least one educational email for every sales email that you send out. The most important thing is to consistently send relevant email content to your subscribers to keep them engaged with your mailing list.

The frequency at which you send broadcast emails will be somewhat dependent upon the niche of your mailing list. For niches that have highly-committed and highly-engaged fans, you will want to email more frequently. Sports fans, investors, and news junkies may want to receive email from you daily because the information in those niches is constantly changing. Niches with hobbyists and casual fans probably won't want to receive email from you on a daily basis. The general rule of thumb that I use for mailing frequency is that you should never mail your list any less than once per week, and you should never mail your list any more than once per day.

Writing a Broadcast Series

If you are launching a new product or running a promotion to generate sales for an existing product, you will want to send a series of emails over the course of several days. When you only send one email about a product or service that you want to promote, your subscribers might miss the email altogether or might simply not have enough information to make a decision. By sending a series of emails over a few days or even a couple of weeks, you are keeping the product or service fresh in their minds. You also have the opportunity to use different selling techniques in the variety of messages you send to your list.

Here is an example layout of how a series of emails can work:

- **Announcement Email (Day 1)** – You first email should serve as an official announcement for the availability of your new product or for the promotion that you're running. Describe what the product does and how it can help your subscribers. If you are running a sale, you should include the discounted pricing information as well as how long the sale will be available.

- **FAQ Email (Day 3)** – The goal of the second email is to provide as much information as possible about the product or promotion to your subscribers. Think of all of the major questions a subscriber might ask about your product or the promotion and answer them in an email. This email can be 1,000 words in length or longer. People that are really interested in your product will take the time to read all of it.

- **Video Tour Email (Day 5)** – Record a YouTube video that shows how your product or service works. If it's a software program or digital information product that you're selling, do a screencast that shows it off. Your email should be little more than a link to watch

your video and a link to purchase the product if the
subscriber is interested. The video that you record will
help visual learners connect with your product more
than they might have otherwise.

- **Features and Benefits Email (Day 7)** – In this email,
  you will remind your subscribers what your product
  does and how it can help them. Write about the
  specific problems that your product can solve for
  them. Include a list of all of the major features of the
  products and how it can benefit them.

- **Social Proof Email (Day 9)** – Collect a few
  testimonials from your existing customers and send
  them out as a way to demonstrate social proof.
  Subscribers will be more likely to buy your product if
  they know that other people like them have already
  purchased your product and gotten value out of it.

- **Warning Email (Day 11)** – In the second-to-last day of
  your campaign, you should try to create a sense of
  urgency and warn subscribers that tomorrow will be
  the last day whatever discount or bonus you are
  offering will be available. You can also use this email
  as another opportunity to remind your subscribers of
  the features and benefits in your product or service.

- **Last Chance Email (Day 12)** – In your final email, you
  should tell your subscribers that it's their last
  opportunity to take advantage of the discount or
  bonus you are offering. Be clear that the price will be
  increasing or the bonus will be going away after
  tonight and that they should act now if they want to
  take advantage of the offer. This email is generally

very short and contains little other than the "last chance" warning and a link to your sales page.

A Sample Email Series from MarketBeat

In order to provide a better idea of what an actual broadcast email series can look like, I've made the copy that I used for an entire email launch available online for free for readers of *Email Marketing Demystified.*

The email series below was for the launch of the new version of our premium daily newsletter that we referred to as "MarketBeat Daily Premium 5.0." The campaign was sent in April 2015 when our mailing list was just under 200,000 subscribers. The campaign generated a total of 91 sales with an expected lifetime value of $299.25 per sale, or $27,231.75 in revenue.

Please note that this campaign was sent before we changed the name of Analyst Ratings Network to MarketBeat, so MarketBeat Daily Premium is referred to by its previous name of ARN Daily Premium. To access the free sample broadcast series, visit mattpaulson.com/sample-campaign.

Tracking Your Results

Some of the broadcast emails that you send your audience will be much more effective than others. It may not be immediately apparent why one email receives better engagement than others, because only by consistently looking at your numbers over time can you begin to identify commonalities between emails that work and those that don't.

Here are the numbers that you should track in every email:

- **Sends** – This is the number of people that your email was sent to. Your number of sends should equal the total size of your mailing list.

- **Bounces** – This is the number of messages that were returned as undeliverable. If your bounce rate is higher than 2%, you may need to clean up the mailing list or your domain name, or your mailing IP address may have been blacklisted.

- **Opens** – This is the number of times your email was opened by subscribers. Note that an open can only be tracked when someone enables images on your messages, so your actual open count will always be higher than your reported open count.

- **Open Rate** – This is the percentage of subscribers that opened an email, out of everyone who received the message. Open rates can vary dramatically based on your industry and the engagement of your mailing list. For well-maintained lists, open rates tend to range from 15% to 35%.

- **Clicks** – This is the total number of subscribers that clicked on a link in your message.

- **Clickthrough Rate** – This is the percentage of people that opened your email, out of everyone that got messaged, and clicked on a link. A good marketing email will have a clickthrough rate of between 5% and 10%.

- **Unsubscribes** – This is the number of people that unsubscribed from your list by clicking on the unsubscribe link in any given email. Seeing a higher-than-usual number of unsubscribes can indicate a message didn't engage well with your mailing list.

There are additional metrics that you should track in sales and marketing emails:

- **Conversions** – This is the number of sales or other sign-ups that occurred as a result of an email.

- **Conversion Rate** – This is the percentage of people that clicked on a link in your email that purchased a product or service as a result of the email.

- **Revenue** – This is how much money you actually made in sales from people clicking through. At the end of the day, the revenue that your email generates is the only metric that matters. However, you should still pay attention to other metrics because they will impact your revenue numbers.

Whenever you send out an email to your mailing list, go back and review how the message performed 72 hours after it was sent. By this time, most of the people that are ever going to read your email will have done so. Compare the open rates, clickthrough rates, and conversion rates to previous emails. Were the numbers significantly higher or lower? If so, try to identify how your current email is different from any previous messages you sent. Ask yourself what you can learn based on the performance of your most recent email.

Create a Weekly or Bi-Weekly Newsletter

One of the best ways to keep your mailing list engaged with your content over time is to publish a weekly or bi-weekly newsletter containing content that is interesting to your readers. By consistently sending a newsletter on a specific day of the week, your subscribers will begin to expect and look forward to your weekly newsletter. They will get in a habit of reading it on a specific day of the week and are more likely to be engaged with your content over time.

Your newsletter should contain five to ten stories or news items that users can scan through and click on to learn more if they are interested. This doesn't mean that you need to write five to ten original articles for your newsletter, though. In fact, you don't actually need to create any new content for your newsletter. You can simply repurpose content that you have recently published to your website for your newsletter.

If you aren't creating original content, you can simply act as a curator and link to interesting stories that your subscribers will be interested in.

For example, Hiten Shah publishes a weekly newsletter for software entrepreneurs called SaaS Weekly (hiten.com), which contains a round-up of stories that are interesting to software entrepreneurs. He doesn't publish any original content in his newsletter but has built a following of more than 11,000 subscribers based on his ability to find interesting stories to share with other software entrepreneurs.

HubSpot has put together an article titled "15 Email Newsletter Examples We Love Getting in Our Inboxes"[19] that shows off several particularly high-quality newsletters. If you need ideas about how to create a newsletter, this is a great place to start.

Marketing Automation for Email

If your company or organization sells a number of different products or has customers with multiple divergent interest areas, you might consider using marketing automation techniques, so customers only receive email content that is relevant to them.

Email marketing automation is the process of sending targeted email content to a certain set of subscribers who have taken a specific action or expressed a specific interest.

In other words, email marketing automation is simply sending the right email to the right person at the right time. By sending more targeted and relevant content to your subscribers based on their interests and actions, they are more likely to stay engaged with your mailing list and buy products and services from your company.

For example, if a customer signs up for a 30-day free trial of a product, they should receive a series of emails (called a campaign) that teaches them how to use that product and sells them on continuing with the product after their 30-day trial is completed.

Obviously, only users that sign up for a free trial of that product should receive those emails, because they would be irrelevant to anyone else. When you send email to people not relevant to them, they will be confused as to the purpose of the message and will likely become disengaged with your content.

There is a lot of upfront work involved with creating marketing automation campaigns. Most email service providers will do the heavy technical lifting for you, but you will need to write an entire series of emails for each campaign that you create and will have to figure out how to trigger a campaign for a specific person when they take an action.

If your mailing list is in a specific niche and you generally only send out content about one or two topics, marketing automation may not be necessary. If your company doesn't sell any products or only sells one or two products or services, email marketing automation might be overkill.

Marketing automation can be an incredibly effective tool, but it may not be worth the effort for smaller and more focused lists.

Here are some types of email marketing automation campaigns that can be very effective:

- **Product Education Emails** – Whenever a new customer buys a product or service from your company, send them a series of emails that teaches them how to use it. This will increase the likelihood that they will actually use and get value from your product. By increasing the percentage of your customers that actually use your product, you are less likely to get refund requests, and customers are more likely to buy from you again in the future.

- **Order Confirmation Emails** – Whenever someone buys a product or service from your company, send an email thanking them for their order along with their order details. You should also provide a call-to-action in this email that will try to get users to return to your website to re-engage with your content or to view related products.

- **Subscriber Re-Engagement Emails** – When a subscriber hasn't opened an email from you or visited your website in a couple of months, send them some highly valuable content to try to get them re-engaged with your content. You can also send an email asking for feedback to see if there's something you can add or change that might engage them more.

- **Anniversary Emails** – Send subscribers a virtual anniversary card after they have been on your mailing list for either six months or one year. You can also include a time-limited coupon for your company's products or services to encourage them to take action and become a customer.

- **Free Trial Emails** – If you offer a service that has a free trial, you should send anyone currently in a trial some information about the product they are using, as well as sales and marketing emails to persuade them to upgrade to a paid subscription.

- **Former Customer Email** – If you run a subscription or a recurring service business, consider creating a campaign that reminds former customers about the features and benefits of your service and allows them to re-register at a discounted rate. These emails work extremely well if written correctly and can prevent you from losing customers forever.

- **Cart Abandonment Emails** – If a customer adds a product to their shopping cart on an ecommerce website but doesn't complete the purchase, send them information about the products in their shopping cart over the next several days. This can be a very effective way to save lost sales.

- **Upsell Emails** – If you have a multi-tiered pricing plan, send an email to customers asking them to upgrade to the next level or service whenever they are about to reach the limitations of their current plan.

List Segmentation

Another aspect of email marketing automation is segmentation. Segmentation is simply the process of breaking up a mailing list into smaller lists—known as segments—based on interests.

If you use an email service provider with marketing automation functionality, you can send an email that allows users to express interest in learning about various topics. Users will click on one or more topics they are interested in, and they will automatically be added to the segments or sub-lists they select. Granted, you may have to email your mailing list multiple times to get a good portion of your subscribers to self-select into different segments. When segmenting your mailing list, you will be sending a larger number of emails in a given month, but each email will only be sent to a specific portion of your list. This will increase the relevance of the emails that you send to any given subscriber.

For example, if you had a blog about building websites, you might have some users that are interested in different content management systems like WordPress, Drupal, and Concrete5. Users that are interested in WordPress might not be interested in getting email about Drupal and Concrete5. If you have a piece of educational content about WordPress you want to send to your mailing list, you might only mail it to the segment of your audience that has expressed interest in learning about WordPress.

Segmentation works best for large mailing lists that have more than 25,000 subscribers and for lists related to broad topics with smaller interest areas. If you have a smaller list, it may not be worth the effort to segment your audience if there will be only a small number of people in any given segment.

If your mailing list is very focused on a single topic, segmentation may not be necessary. You should identify between three and six interest areas to use as segments of your mailing list. If you try to create too many, you may end up with very small segments that aren't big enough to be worth mailing individually.

Wrap-Up

While developing a plan to regularly email your mailing list through your autoresponder series and through broadcast emails may seem like a big chore, it doesn't have to be. Start simply by writing your welcome email and the first few emails in your autoresponder series. Continue to add a new email to it every couple of days until it's complete.

As your first subscribers begin to complete the series, start sending periodic broadcast emails to your list to ensure that all of your subscribers are regularly getting email from you. Over time, consider more advanced strategies like list segmentation and marketing automation to maximize the effectiveness of your email marketing efforts.

Action Steps

- Write your welcome email and enter it into your email service provider.

- Write your first three autoresponder emails and add them into your email service provider.

- Create a schedule of all of the broadcast emails you want to send to your list next month.

- Consider sending a weekly newsletter to your subscribers.

- Track the performance of every email that you send.

Chapter Five

Writing Email That Inspires Users to Take Action

You have undoubtedly written thousands of emails in your life. You probably regularly send and receive email from friends, family, coworkers, and even complete strangers on a regular basis for any number of reasons. While writing an email to any one person is a straightforward proposition, sending an email to a large group of people is an entirely different skillset. You need to craft a message that attracts the attention of a diverse group of individuals, clearly communicates a single objective, and inspires them to take a desired action. If that doesn't sound hard enough, you have to do this without the use of video, audio, images (sometimes), and other dynamic content. You also have to deal with the technical peculiarities of email, avoid spam filters, and maintain compliance with your country's anti-spam laws. Writing effective email is both an art and a science. This chapter will show you how to write email copy that engages users and convinces them to take action.

Understanding Your Audience

In order to effectively write to your audience, you first have to understand who they are. How old are your typical subscribers? What do they do for a living? What gender are they? Are they married? Where do they live? What are their interests? What problems do they face? Why did they sign up for your mailing list? If you don't know these things, conduct a survey and ask people to share information about themselves, so you have a better idea of who is actually receiving your email.

I recommend creating a fictional character that epitomizes your typical customer, known as an avatar. The character that you create should have a name, an age, a gender, a job, a hometown, personal interests, and problems that they face on a daily basis. The avatar that I created for MarketBeat is named Bill. He is about fifty years old. He's married, is a homeowner, and has some money to invest in the stock market. He likes to pick his own stocks but isn't sure whose advice he should listen to. He can live just about anywhere in the United States or Canada and loves to keep up with the day-to-day news in the stock market. By creating an avatar, you will have a better idea of who you are marketing to and, in many ways, can get inside the minds of your subscribers.

When you write an email to your mailing list, write as if you are sending a personal message to your avatar. Ask yourself what your avatar would need to hear in order to take action based on your email. What kind of hopes do they have that you can encourage? What kind of fears do they have that you can assuage? If you write to your avatar and use lots of "you" language, subscribers will subconsciously think that your email was written to them specifically and will be more likely to engage with your message. Keep the focus on your subscribers as much as possible. Make your emails about them, not about you.

Here's an example of an email that uses personal language:

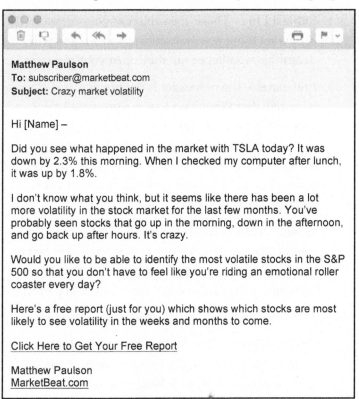

Matthew Paulson
To: subscriber@marketbeat.com
Subject: Crazy market volatility

Hi [Name] –

Did you see what happened in the market with TSLA today? It was down by 2.3% this morning. When I checked my computer after lunch, it was up by 1.8%.

I don't know what you think, but it seems like there has been a lot more volatility in the stock market for the last few months. You've probably seen stocks that go up in the morning, down in the afternoon, and go back up after hours. It's crazy.

Would you like to be able to identify the most volatile stocks in the S&P 500 so that you don't have to feel like you're riding an emotional roller coaster every day?

Here's a free report (just for you) which shows which stocks are most likely to see volatility in the weeks and months to come.

Click Here to Get Your Free Report

Matthew Paulson
MarketBeat.com

Parts of an Email

When getting ready to put together an email, it would be easy to think that the only thing you have to write is the message body. However, there are actually several different components of every message that you send to your list. You need to put as much thought and effort into the other parts of your email as you would in the main message body.

Here are the key components of an email:

- **Subject Line** – This is the subject of your message. It is the first thing your subscribers will see and will determine whether or not they open your message.

- **Preheader** – The preheader is the preview text included after the subject line in some email services, such as Gmail. It can serve as a second subject line that will further encourage users to open your email. If you don't intentionally add a preheader, most email services will use the first sentence or two of your email as a preheader.

- **"From" Name** – This is the name of the person sending the email. Use your personal name in lieu of the name of your company, because email users are more likely to open an email from an actual person.

- **Message Body** – This is the main text of your email.

- **Call-to-Action** – This is a hyperlink at the bottom of your message body that persuades users to take a specific action, such as clicking on a hyperlink.

- **Signature** – Keep your email signature simple. Long email signatures can be a distraction to the main content of your email. I personally just use my name on one line and the name of my company on the following line.

- **Postscript** – Consider periodically using a "P.S." below your email signature to serve as a secondary sales tool after your main email. For example, you could include something like, "P.S. Remember that our service comes with a 30-day money-back guarantee. If you're not satisfied with our service within the first 30 days, just let us know, and we'll provide you a full refund."

- **Footer** – Your footer usually contains your unsubscribe link and other information that you need to include to stay compliant with anti-spam laws, such as your mailing address and the name of your company. Your footer will likely be the same for every email that you send to your list.

Types of Messages

Every email that you send to your mailing list will be sent for a specific purpose. You might have an announcement to make or want your subscribers to read a piece of content you recently posted. You may want them to check out one of your company's products or keep them engaged by sending them helpful information.

Here are some of the main reasons that you will email your list:

- **Announcements** – Whenever you have something big to announce, you should announce it to your email subscribers, so they know they are valued members of your community.

- **Sales and Marketing** – You will periodically want to send sales and marketing emails to your subscribers about your company's products and services. Make sure you only email subscribers about a product or a sale they haven't already purchased.

- **Affiliate Marketing** – In order to generate additional revenue, you can promote another company's products and services as an affiliate. Read the monetization chapter of this book for more information about how to do this.

- **Weekly Newsletter** – Consider creating a weekly newsletter for your subscribers that contains useful and interesting content. Your weekly newsletter will help keep users interested and engaged with your content.

- **User Engagement** – You will want to regularly send your subscribers valuable tips, resources, and other helpful information that will keep them engaged with your mailing list.

- **Feedback** – Whenever you need feedback about an idea, email your audience and ask them for it. Ask two or three questions and request they respond with their feedback by replying.

- **List Management** – You may need to periodically send messages to users relating to the status of their subscription. You might need to reconfirm their subscription if they haven't opened an email from you in a while, or you might want them to identify specific interests as part of a segmentation campaign.

Give, Give, Give, Ask

While you will email your audience for many different reasons, you need to keep a healthy balance between sending emails that provide value to your audience and emails that take value away.

Emails that contain information helpful to your readers at no cost to them, such as tips, educational content, resources, and training videos, *provide* value to your audience. Emails that ask your audience to purchase a product or take action that benefits you more than them will *take* value from your audience.

I recommend sending at least two emails that provide value to your audience for every one email that takes it from them. Ideally, you will provide so much value to your audience that they respond to your sales and marketing emails out of sheer gratitude for the value you have already provided. This principle is outlined in detail by Gary Vaynerchuk in his book, *Jab, Jab, Jab, Right Hook: How to Tell Your Story in a Noisy Social World.*

Writing Great Subject Lines

Your subject lines are the most important words that you will write as part of your email marketing strategy. If you write a subject line that is uninspired and doesn't grab the attention of your subscribers, they probably aren't going to open your message.

According to a report from Chadwick Martin Bailey, 64% of people say they will choose to open an email because of the subject line.[20] If you write a great subject line, you'll receive higher open rates, which will lead to more clickthroughs and more sales. A well-written subject line can often receive double the open rates of a poorly-written one, which will in turn double your clickthroughs and double the sales generated by an email.

Here are some examples of a few different types of subject lines that you can use:

- **Confrontation:** Quit Wasting Your Time With Options Trading
- **Curiosity:** Strange Question…?
- **How to:** How to Double Your Revenue With One Little-Known Email Marketing Technique
- **Humor:** Forget Black Friday – Enjoy Wine Weekend
- **Numbers:** What 83% of Golfers Screw Up on the Course
- **Reply-To:** RE: Your Subscription to MarketBeat Daily Premium
- **Shocking:** How I Lost 48 Pounds in ONE WEEK
- **Testimonial:** "MarketBeat made me $12,384.32 in one trade"
- **Time Sensitive:** Tonight's Deadline (Last Chance!)
- **Tips:** 3 Ways to Double Your Facebook Following
- **Warning:** Don't Miss Out!

Here are some of the subject lines that have received the highest open-rates in the history of MarketBeat:

- An important reminder… (40.8% open rate)
- RE: Clean Water Project (27.6% open rate)

- I'm Sorry :\ (27.1% open rate)

- Bad News (25% open rate)

- Good News! :-) (24% open rate)

- Clearing up some confusion (24.6% open rate)

- Important (please read) (23.9% open rate)

- Black Friday...in June? (21.9% open rate)

- Weird Question? (21.4% open rate)

There are also a number of techniques that can modify subject lines to emphasize words and to make unsaid promises about the content of your message. If you are going to use any variation techniques (listed below), switch them up from email to email, and don't use any one technique more than twice each month. Subscribers will notice these patterns if used too often, rendering them ineffective.

Here are the techniques:

- **Make an Email Appear Personal** – Make your entire subject line lowercase to imply that the message is personal in nature, because individuals don't always put the same effort into writing an error-free and correctly-capitalized subject line. For example, "how I beat the stock market" sounds a lot more personal than "How I Beat the Stock Market."

- **Imply Strong Emotion and Importance** – You can uppercase your subject line to imply strong emotion or importance to your email. For example, "I BEAT THE STOCK MARKET" implies urgency and importance.

- **Specific Numbers** – You can use specific numbers, like 23.6 or 29%, to imply accuracy of your data. People are naturally wired to think that numbers are less likely to be fabricated if they are more specific or have a decimal point. For example, "How I Beat the Market by 7.8% in 2015" would imply that there's more math showing how I beat the stock market by that *exact* number.

- **Emphasize** – You can emphasize a particular word by uppercasing only that word or by surrounding that word with asterisks. For example, "How I BEAT the Stock Market by 7.8% When Others Failed" draws attention to the word "beat."

- **More Information Inside** – You can add ellipses (three periods) at the end of your subject line to imply that there's much more for users inside of your email. For example, "How I beat the stock market..." implies that I will share details in the body of the email.

- **Communicate Two Things at Once** – Use brackets when you need to communicate two different things about an email. For example, "How I Beat the Stock Market [Free Video]" implies that users will both learn how to beat the stock market and get a free video in their inbox.

Don't believe that you have to write every email subject line from scratch. Feel free to use the subject lines listed in this chapter. You can get good ideas for subject lines by searching for "subject line ideas" in your search engine of choice.

I also recommend signing up for the mailing lists of well-known Internet marketers like Frank Kern, Eben Pagan, and Ryan Deiss so that you can see how entrepreneurs that make millions of dollars each year perform their craft.

Writing an Announcement Email

Periodically, you'll have a new project or some other news that you want to share with your mailing list. It will be very tempting to write an email that communicates how excited you are for your project and how it's going to change your business. Remember that your audience cares about themselves much more than they care about you, so always make announcements in such a way that keeps the focus on your subscribers.

Your announcement email should also attempt to generate excitement and enthusiasm in your subscribers by suggesting how your announcement can change their lives. Finally, don't write something vague that's filled with a lot of hype and doesn't actually tell your subscribers the specifics of what you want to announce. Be clear and concise about the details of your announcement in your email.

Here's an example of an announcement email I might send to MarketBeat subscribers:

Matthew Paulson
To: subscriber@marketbeat.com
Subject: Something New from MarketBeat

Hey [Name] –

There have been a lot of ups and downs in the market recently. Some of your stocks are probably doing quite well, and there are others that you might want to sweep under the rug.

You've really got to pick out strong companies with good fundamentals in order to ride out the waves of a volatile market.

If you'd like help identifying a few great companies with good fundamentals to add to your portfolio, we've developed a brand new screening tool that will allow you to find companies that are poised to appreciate by more than 10% over the next 12 months through some newly-developed, advanced trading algorithms that hedge funds don't even have access to.

We've found one company that has a potential upside of more than 35%. Now, wouldn't that be a nice return to brag about on the golf course?

We call this new tool the MarketBeat Volatility Opportunity Screener, and it's included free with your existing subscription to RatingsDB.

Click Here to Access the MarketBeat Volatility Screener

Thanks!

Matthew Paulson
MarketBeat.com

Writing an Affiliate Marketing Email

If you are promoting another company's product or service in exchange for an affiliate commission, you are personally endorsing that product or service, and that should be reflected in your email. When writing an affiliate marketing email, communicate the features and benefits of the product you are promoting. Make it clear how the product can help your subscribers specifically and always disclose that you are getting paid to help the company generate sales.

Here is an example of an affiliate marketing email I might send:

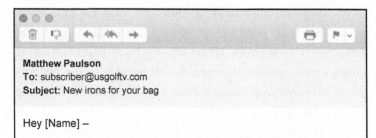

Matthew Paulson
To: subscriber@usgolftv.com
Subject: New irons for your bag

Hey [Name] –

With the spring golf season just two months away, it's hard to not start salivating over the opportunity to get on the course. If you're like me, you've probably already dusted off your golf bag, cleaned up your clubs, and gotten everything else ready for the season. I think what I'm most excited about for this year's golf season is my brand new set of irons from XYZ Golf.

I was down in Florida a month or so back, and a buddy had an early set of the new XYZ irons. They have some of the best grips I've ever seen and have a newly-designed clubhead specially made to increase both speed and accuracy. They also have this amazing little wedge that has gotten me out of the sand on 100% of the shots I've taken. There are a lot of iron clubs on the market right now, but I really think the XYZ clubs are the ones to beat.

In fact, XYZ irons are so good that I want to make sure you can get your set ahead of the season. XYZ's generally not in stores yet, but I've found one retailer that has 40 full sets she's ready to sell for just $299.97 apiece. I don't think you'll be able to find a better price anywhere else.

If you'd like to check out the new XYZ irons, click on the link below. I also want to let you know that I will receive a small commission if you purchase using the link below, but I wouldn't ever recommend a product or service that I wouldn't use personally.

Click Here to Get Your XYZ Irons

Matthew Paulson
USGolfTV

Writing Content Promotion Emails

If you create a new resource, such as a very long blog post, a new podcast episode, or a new ebook, send an email to your audience letting them know it's available. Don't assume your subscribers will read every blog post on your website, because that rarely happens. When you have a great new piece of content for them to consume, let them know via email, so they won't miss it and will stay engaged with your mailing list. If you want your subscribers to promote your content, use a bit of the social capital you have built up with them, and ask them to share your content. Remember to include links so that a subscriber can easily share your post on Facebook as well.

Here's an example of a content promotion email I might send:

Matthew Paulson
To: subscriber@marketbeat.com
Subject: New resource for aspiring entrepreneurs

Good Morning –

One of the hardest challenges that every new entrepreneur makes is taking the leap and acquiring their first customer. Many new entrepreneurs get distracted by working on their name, building their website, creating business cards, reading business books, and going to conferences. While these things can be fun to do, none of these things actually help your business generate revenue.

I've always wondered why new entrepreneurs don't just start identifying prospects, setting up meetings, and trying to get sales. I had a discussion the other day with a newer entrepreneur, and he told me that he doesn't actually know how to make a sales call to ask for a meeting. Certainly, some new entrepreneurs don't make sales calls because they are afraid of being rejected, but others simply don't know how to generate sales.

If you want to learn the exact steps you need to take and the right words to say to identify a new prospect, get a sales meeting with them, and close the deal, I've developed a brand new 5,000-word blog post just for you. It's titled "The Five Steps of Customer Prospecting: What To Do and What to Say," and it's available at the link below.

Click Here to Read "The Five Steps of Customer Prospecting"

Enjoy!

Matthew Paulson
Founder, MarketBeat.com

Learn How to Make a Sales Call Here

Writing Feedback Emails

Market research is one of the best uses for your mailing list. Nobody knows more about what your subscribers actually want than your subscribers themselves. Whenever you are thinking about launching a new product, a new service, or creating another resource for them, always ask for feedback ahead of time. People love to share their opinions with strangers, so you'll probably receive a lot of responses if you take the time to ask for feedback. Only ask a few questions at a time and leave the questions open-ended, so they have room to tell you what they really think.

Here is an example of a feedback email that I might send:

Matthew Paulson
To: subscriber@marketbeat.com
Subject: Quick question?

Hi [Name] –

As a subscriber to MarketBeat Daily Premium and RatingsDB, you've had access to analyst ratings changes, earnings announcements, and insider trades well before the market opens each morning.

We're getting ready to start on the next round of improvements to our services, and I wanted to get your feedback before we started. If you could take a moment to provide your thoughts and insight, I would be immensely grateful.

Here are the questions:

#1 – What do you like most about our services? What do you like the least?

#2 – Do you feel that MarketBeat Daily Premium is too cluttered? What could be removed?

#3 – Do you have any ideas or suggestions to improve our daily newsletter or our research software?

If you'd be willing to help, simply reply to this email with your feedback.

Thanks in advance,

Matthew Paulson
Founder, MarketBeat.com

Writing Sales and Marketing Emails with AIDA

In order to write an effective sales and marketing email, you need to take your subscribers through a series of steps to get them to take a desired action, such as purchasing a product or service. You first have to grab their **attention**, create **interest** in your product or service, instill a personal **desire** for your offer using your subscribers' hopes and fears, and convince them to take **action**. These four steps make up the acronym AIDA, which was first penned by advertising pioneer E. St. Elmo Lewis in 1903. While the concept AIDA was developed in the print era, it continues to work well as a framework for email copywriting.

The first step is to grab the **attention** of your readers. In the world of email marketing, this means getting your subscribers to see and open your email. Your subscribers may receive as many as one hundred emails every day. They probably do not read most of the emails they receive and may only open five to ten messages on any given day. This is why some of the most engaged email lists in the world only have open rates of 30-40%. In order to actually get consumers to open your emails, you need to stand apart from the crowd by writing a compelling subject line and using a personal "from" name. After someone has opened your email, keep their attention by telling an interesting story, fact, joke, or anything else that someone can't help but read.

After getting a subscriber's attention, you will need to smoothly transition to the actual purpose of your email, so you can generate **interest** for the product or service you're promoting. You can often do this through an analogy that ties the content of your email back into the introduction you used to grab their attention. After the transition, you will extol the features and benefits of what you are selling your audience, and show them how it can solve a particular problem for them or make their lives easier.

The next step is to create an emotional **desire** in your subscribers. Try to get your users to think about the emotions they feel whenever they face the particular problem that your product or service can solve. Also, paint a picture of a desired future state that subscribers can achieve when they purchase your product or service. By helping them remember the negative emotions caused by the problem and showing them what their life can be like if they purchase your product or service to solve it, you will help your customers become emotionally ready to purchase.

The final step is to call your subscribers to take a specific **action,** which is usually purchasing your product or service. Tell your subscribers exactly what they need to do to purchase your product, and finish your email by reminding users of the picture you painted of a desired future state.

Here's an example of a marketing email that was sent out by USGolfTV that uses AIDA:

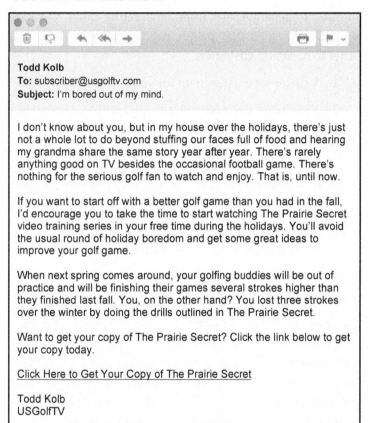

Todd Kolb
To: subscriber@usgolftv.com
Subject: I'm bored out of my mind.

I don't know about you, but in my house over the holidays, there's just not a whole lot to do beyond stuffing our faces full of food and hearing my grandma share the same story year after year. There's rarely anything good on TV besides the occasional football game. There's nothing for the serious golf fan to watch and enjoy. That is, until now.

If you want to start off with a better golf game than you had in the fall, I'd encourage you to take the time to start watching The Prairie Secret video training series in your free time during the holidays. You'll avoid the usual round of holiday boredom and get some great ideas to improve your golf game.

When next spring comes around, your golfing buddies will be out of practice and will be finishing their games several strokes higher than they finished last fall. You, on the other hand? You lost three strokes over the winter by doing the drills outlined in The Prairie Secret.

Want to get your copy of The Prairie Secret? Click the link below to get your copy today.

Click Here to Get Your Copy of The Prairie Secret

Todd Kolb
USGolfTV

The Six Steps to Generating a Sale from Email Marketing

In order to generate sales from a marketing email, there are six different steps that people need to take in sequential order to become a customer:

1. A customer must sign up for your mailing list.

2. A customer must become engaged with your content and read the emails you sent.

3. A customer must receive and open a marketing email.

4. A customer must click a link in your marketing email to your sales page.

5. A customer must read the sales material for your product or service on your landing page.

6. A customer must take action and purchase your product.

As email subscribers work through the six steps of becoming a customer, many of them are going to drop off the map and will never become customers. Furthermore, they will likely drop out at different points along the way. All of your subscribers will make it through step one. Half might make it through step two. Around 15% of your subscribers might make it through step three, 5% might make it through step four, while 3% of your subscribers might make it through step five. Finally, 2% of your subscribers might make it through step six.

The key is to get as many subscribers as possible from one step to the next. If subscribers drop off at *any* particular point in these six steps, they will never become customers. You should work on optimizing all six of these steps to ensure the highest percentage of subscribers possible make it from any one step to the next step. The best method is continually running split-tests at every step of the process. By trying different opt-in forms, email marketing copy, subject lines, calls-to-action, and landing page copy over time, you'll identify the language that will help drive more sales.

Best Practices to Follow With Your Email

There are several other best practices that you should follow when sending email to your list:

- **Don't Rely on Images** – Between 10% and 30% of your users will never click "enable images" on your emails. Never rely on images to convey key points in your copy. Use clear and descriptive ALT text on any images that you do include. You can also consider using CSS styling to make your ALT text larger and more visible to subscribers that do not enable images.

- **Avoid Grammar and Spelling Errors** – Poor grammar, capitalization, and spelling can be a huge turn off for many of your email subscribers. If you want to speak with expert authority to your audience, you need to do so with proper, clear writing. No one will believe you are an authority on anything if you can't write a complete sentence. Double-check every email you write for grammar and spelling mistakes, and consider having another person check over your messages before they are sent out to your subscribers.

- **Include Multiple Hyperlinks** – If you have a specific link you want users to click on, add a total of three hyperlinks to each email. Hyperlink your main call-to-action at the bottom of your message body and just above your email signature. Also hyperlink a few relevant words in the first paragraph of your email to the page you want users to go to. Finally, include a final call-to-action below your email signature and in any "P.S." that you include with your email.

- **Avoid Design-Heavy Email Templates** – Subscribers are more likely to actually read email that comes from an individual person than a faceless company or nonprofit. While companies frequently use templates in their email, *people* almost never do. If possible, avoid using a design-heavy template so that your emails appear more personal to your subscribers.

- **Limit Each Email to One Call-to-Action** – Don't try to get your subscribers to do multiple things as a result of any one email. Each email that you send should have one single purpose and a single call-to-action that you want them to take. Users are less likely to respond when they have to consider which, if any, of your calls-to-action that they want to take.

- **Have a Clear Unsubscribe Link** – Don't try to hide or obscure your unsubscribe link. Have a clear unsubscribe link that says "Click Here to Unsubscribe" in a normal font size. If you try to obscure your unsubscribe link, your subscribers may report your messages as spam, which can put you in jeopardy with your email service provider if your account generates too many spam complaints.

Should I Hire a Professional Copywriter?

There are many professional email copywriters that you can pay to create email marketing campaigns on your behalf. However, you probably should *not* hire one, especially if you are just getting started. Learning to become an effective copywriter takes experience. When someone else is writing copy for you, you won't have the opportunity to practice and learn how to write your copy for yourself. Good copywriters can be very expensive to hire, which will make it much more difficult to run a profitable email marketing campaign.

There are two instances where it might be appropriate to hire a professional copywriter to write email for you.

If your business is already generating more than six figures per year when you start email marketing, it may be more cost-effective for you to hire a copywriter. At $200,000 per year, your time is worth about $150.00 per hour. If it takes you three hours to write an email and a copywriter can do a better job than you at $150.00 per message, go ahead and write a check to the copywriter.

The other instance is for creating your autoresponder series, but only if you don't have much experience writing email, and you can easily afford the fees. By having a professional copywriter create your autoresponder series, you'll have relevant email copy that you can repurpose as broadcast emails down the line.

Wrap-Up

In this chapter, I've put together a basic overview of email copywriting and a list of best practices to follow when writing email to your subscribers. Copywriting is a skill that will take a lot of time and practice to master. Most of the email that you send for the first several months won't be very good, and that's okay. Continue learning and practicing email copywriting by following experts like John McIntyre (themcmethod.com), reading marketing email sent out by your competitors, and consuming educational content about copywriting from places like Copyblogger (copyblogger.com/blog). Over time, your copywriting skills will improve and mature, and you, too, will become America's next great email copywriter.

Action Steps:

- Create an avatar that epitomizes a typical subscriber.

- Practice writing sales and marketing emails using AIDA.

- Know the eight parts of every email and the seven reasons to email your list.

- Identify additional copywriting resources that you can learn from and rely on in the future.

Case Study #4

USGolfTV

USGolfTV is a digital publishing and television production company based out of Sioux Falls, South Dakota. It was founded in 2010 by Todd Kolb, who is a PGA teaching professional. Todd is responsible for content creation and general business strategy. Tyler Prins, another equity partner, is the general manager of the business and handles its day-to-day operations. I acquired a stake in the company in August 2014 and am primarily responsible for marketing and revenue generation.

The business is made up of three primary components: the USGolfTV TV show, the company's video training products, and the company's website (usgolftv.com). The television show, USGolfTV, is a regionally syndicated program that is available in about 12 million homes in 25 states through a variety of cable channels, including Cox, Time Warner, and

Midco Sports Net. The show provides golf tips, product reviews, and industry trends. It makes a minor profit, but its real value is that it gives us a substantial amount of credibility whenever we approach a potential advertiser. Because we can give advertisers exposure on television, in our email newsletter, and on our website, advertisers are much more likely to entertain an initial conversation with us.

The second major component of the business is the company's video training products. USGolfTV has produced three web-based video-training courses that help golfers improve a specific part of their game. We promote these products primarily through email marketing and working with affiliates. On our website, we use a popup opt-in form to get new subscribers to opt in to a 5-day video course which will teach them about a specific part of golf, like putting. After they receive the five videos in the series, they will receive marketing emails for the full premium video course associated with the 5-day course. When you buy one of the premium video courses, you'll get a series of videos featuring Todd in addition to written instructions to help you implement what you're learning on the course. These videos are sold and delivered through a piece of software called ClickFunnels (clickfunnels.com), which serves as both as a landing page service and a product delivery service. These video training products costs between $27.00 and $235.00 depending on which program you buy.

The final component of the business is the USGolfTV website, which serves as the glue that brings all of the other parts of the business together. We have a team of 5-7 writers that publish golf news, product reviews, and other content on USGolfTV.com. We receive traffic from all of the usual sources, including organic searches, social media, and news portals like Google News. We generate revenue on the website through Google AdSense, through private sponsorships, and by gathering email sign-ups, so we can promote our paid products to our audience. The economics of selling our own products on our website are astonishing. We know that 5%-10% of visitors will sign up for a free course on the website, and 3% of those people will buy one of our premium courses that has an average sale price of $100.00, so we can take those numbers and say we expect to make between $200 and $250 from every 1,000 visitors on our website through email marketing alone.

USGolfTV has done a few things with email marketing particularly well. The company regularly does email swaps with a number of different partners in the golf industry to promote our mailing list and our products. We also periodically pay to be featured on another owner's email list to grow our own mailing list and sell our products. USGolfTV has even traded commercial space on our television show in exchange for email sends. The golf industry is very much built on relationships, and our team has leveraged that reality by using our existing relationships to attract affiliates and do email swaps.

USGolfTV uses a popup opt-in form on its website similar to the one used by MarketBeat. We know that customers are more likely to purchase our paid video courses if they opt in to multiple free video series, so we rotate our lead magnets on a daily basis. If one video series isn't useful to a reader, the series that gets promoted the next day might be more interesting to them. The website also includes a number of in-post lead forms to promote specific lead magnets that are tied to the content of the post. We do not run a co-registration ad on our "thank you" page, however, because co-registration ads haven't taken off on sports websites yet. We do place a display advertisement unit on our "thank you" pages, which does quite well.

The USGolfTV website receives about 80,000 unique visitors and 125,000 page views each month. As of October 2015, the company has a mailing list of about 50,000 subscribers and is adding between 4,000 and 5,000 new subscribers each month. While I'm not permitted to disclose exact revenue numbers for this business, it will generate well into six figures in revenue in 2015.

Chapter Six

Monetization: Six Ways to Make Money with Your Mailing List

Building a mailing list does not serve any purpose if it does not also accomplish business objectives. If you run a for-profit company, your ultimate goal is to generate new revenue and get more customers through your email marketing efforts. This chapter will teach you how to sell more of your company's products and services through email marketing and how to generate additional revenue through email advertising networks and through affiliate marketing.

Sell Your Own Products

Most companies use their mailing lists to market their own products and services. If someone comes to your website and completes an opt-in form, they have already expressed interest in your content and are probably a potential customer for your company's products and services. Send emails that educate and inform your subscribers about your products and services regularly. Don't assume that your subscribers already know about what you have to offer, because not everyone pays equal attention to all of the emails you send, and new subscribers are being added to your mailing list regularly.

If you do have products or services that you can sell to your mailing list, you are probably better off promoting your own products than another company's products, even those you would receive an affiliate commission for promoting. When you sell your own products and services, you get to keep 100% of the customer's payment. When you are promoting someone else's product, you may receive as little as 10% of the revenue generated by a sale.

If you don't have any products or services that you can sell to your audience, consider making a course that teaches something to your subscribers or helps them achieve a specific goal. While the product creation and launch process is beyond the scope of this book, read my earlier book, *40 Rules for Internet Business Success*, for advice on how to create and market your first product. You can also read Jeff Walker's book, *Launch,* for additional guidance on the process of launching your first product.

Here are some strategies that you can use to generate sales for your company's product or service.

- **Use Your Autoresponder Series** – Sprinkle information about your company's products and services in your autoresponder series. Subscribers are often most engaged with your mailing list soon after they first subscribe, so don't wait more than a week or two before sending them sales and marketing material.

- **Run a Sale** – Periodically, consider offering a time-limited discount on one of your company's products or services to generate additional sales. Offer a 20-30% discount on whatever you are promoting, but only make that discount available for a fixed period of time, such as three, five, or seven days. Send multiple emails during the sale that extol the features and benefits of your company's products and services. On the last day of the sale, send your subscribers an email reminding them of the deal and making it clear the sale is ending that night. By having a hard deadline for your sale, potential customers who are on the fence will be more likely to take action to avoid missing the sale.

- **Offer Special Bonuses** – Another way to add urgency to the purchasing process is offering a special bonus to customers that purchase by a specific date. It can be another of your products or a small add-on product that you create to serve specifically as a bonus. At MarketBeat, we frequently use a 50-page investment guide we put together as a bonus that's not otherwise available. A special bonus campaign will operate very similar to a sale campaign, because subscribers will be getting something they wouldn't otherwise normally receive and have to take action by a specific date and time.

- **Relaunch Existing Products** – If you have a product that you launched more than a year ago, consider adding some new features and benefits and launching it to your mailing list as a "new and improved" version of your product. The new version of your product will provide a great excuse to execute an email marketing campaign as if you were launching a new product, and subscribers will take a second look at a product they might have otherwise ignored. Make sure you give all of your existing customers a free upgrade to the new version to avoid any hard feelings. You can make a relaunch campaign more effective by offering a sale or a special bonus during the launch period to your subscribers.

- **Group Products Together** – If your company offers complimentary products and services, consider creating a campaign where customers can buy two products at once for a single price. You should offer a slight discount for the combined product offering, and consider adding a bonus that's only available to people who purchase both products in a package.

- **Create New Products** – If your existing products and services aren't getting the sales traction with your mailing list that they once were, you can always create a new product. At USGolfTV, we regularly launch new premium video training courses so that we have fresh products and content to promote to our audience. When you have a new product, you can create buzz with a pre-launch marketing campaign and generate a level of interest that you otherwise might not be able to when marketing an existing product.

At MarketBeat, we use our mailing list to sell subscription information services to our subscriber base. Specifically, we sell a piece of investment research software called RatingsDB and a premium daily newsletter called MarketBeat Daily Premium.

Through our daily newsletter, our autoresponder series, and broadcast emails that we send to our mailing list, we are able to generate more than $500,000 per year in recurring annual revenue from the subscription products we sell. We also regularly launch new products, relaunch existing products, and offer time-limited discounts and bonuses for customers that buy during campaigns.

Promote Third-Party Products and Services as an Affiliate

There are thousands of companies that will pay you commissions for any sales that you generate on their behalf, an arrangement known in the online business world as affiliate marketing. Promoting other companies' products and services to your mailing list can be an extremely effective way to generate revenue if you can find one that is a great match for your audience.

Even if your company produces its own products and services, you should still consider promoting other companies. You can only talk about your products so much before your audience gets sick of hearing about them.

Finding Products to Promote

Finding products and services to promote as an affiliate is an incredibly straightforward process. There are several large advertising networks that focus exclusively on creating affiliate relationships between advertisers and publishers. These networks will handle any necessary paperwork, provide banners and other creative tools to use on your website, serve as an intermediary in the relationship, and make sure you get paid for your efforts.

Affiliate networks also make it very easy to find products and services to promote. They will list advertisers by category and show which advertisers other publishers are currently having the most success with.

Commission Junction (cj.com), a large affiliate advertising network, currently has nearly 3,000 different advertisers listed. Keep in mind that you will have the most success promoting products closely related to the content that you write about. If you had a website about investing, you would primarily want to promote investing-related services like stock brokerages and stock research tools. You wouldn't get good results promoting unrelated services like web hosting and domain name registration services.

Here is a list of some of the larger affiliate advertising networks:

- Amazon Associates (affiliate-program.amazon.com)
- Click Bank (clickbank.com)
- Commission Junction (cj.com)
- eBay Partner Network (ebaypartnernetwork.com)
- Flex Offers (flexoffers.com)

- LinkShare (linkshare.com)
- ShareASale (shareasale.com)
- VigLink (viglink.com)

If you are overwhelmed by the sheer number of advertisers that list their products on affiliate networks, you can simplify the process by looking at what products and services your competitors and other similar websites are promoting. If several other websites are all promoting a specific advertiser and they have been for several months, there's a good chance they are making good money promoting them.

To identify which network a particular advertiser is using, simply do a web search for the name of the advertiser followed by the word "affiliate program," and the sign-up link will appear more often than not.

How Does an Affiliate Marketing Email Actually Work?

After you have found an advertiser that you want to promote and have signed up for their affiliate program through an advertising network, you will be given hyperlinks to use that will track any sales you generate. They may also provide an image tag that serves as a tracking pixel to include in your email.

You will write a sales and marketing email to your audience as you normally would for your company's products and services. Then use the hyperlink they provided you as the hyperlink in your call-to-action so that sales are properly tracked. If they provided a tracking pixel, place it in your

HTML at the bottom of your email, so the number of times the offer was viewed can be properly tracked by the affiliate program.

How Much Can I Make Through Affiliate Marketing?

With affiliate marketing, payments are made based on the actual sales that you generate. The amount of money you can make through affiliate marketing depends on a number of factors, including the size of your list, the relevance of the product or service to your list, and the effectiveness of the marketing copy that you use to write a product. If you have a small list and are ineffectively promoting a product that's not relevant to your list, you probably won't make anything through affiliate marketing.

If you have a larger list of highly-engaged subscribers who trust your recommendations and you can promote a product or service that's very relevant to your audience, you can make tens of thousands of dollars per month. If you have a list of a few thousand subscribers, you will probably earn $100-$200 per month through affiliate marketing for the first several months. Your revenue will steadily increase over time as your list grows and as you identify products and services to promote that are a good match for your list.

What Best Practices Should I Follow as an Affiliate?

There are several best practices that you should follow when promoting products and services to your audience as an affiliate:

- **Be Transparent** – You should always disclose to your subscribers if you are receiving a commission for promoting a product or service for honesty, transparency, and even legal reasons. In the United States, the FTC requires that you disclose any payment that you receive for endorsing a product or service. You can read the FTC's endorsement guidelines at 1.usa.gov/1FRMynQ.

- Promotion **Equals Endorsement** – If you are promoting a product as an affiliate, you are personally endorsing that product as something your subscribers should use. If you wouldn't personally use a product or service, don't promote it to your mailing list. Your subscribers will lose trust in you if you promote low-quality products and are only concerned with the affiliate commissions you generate.

- **Don't Over-Promote One Product** – You will see diminishing returns after you continue to promote the same product over time. Rotate the products and services that you promote to avoid overexposing any one advertiser to your mailing list.

- **Include a Bonus** – To ensure a subscriber signs up for something through your affiliate link, create a bonus product that's only available to those who sign up through your affiliate link. You can use one of your existing products or create an educational piece of content to serve as your bonus. Have subscribers forward you the welcome email or the receipt that they get from the advertiser in exchange for the bonus product you create.

- **Follow Program Rules** – Each affiliate advertiser will have their own set of program rules. They may place limitations on the language that you use and the ways that you promote their product or service. Take the time to read the rules set by each advertiser to avoid having your relationship terminated through inadvertently breaking one of their program rules.

Pat Flynn (smartpassiveincome.com) is a great example of someone who does affiliate marketing properly through email, his website, and his podcast. He has established himself as an online business expert and recommends tools, products, and services to his audience that can help them build their online businesses. He only promotes products that he can personally recommend and is always transparent when he receives an affiliate commission for promoting something. He has built such a large audience, and his affiliate marketing is so effective that the commissions he generates through his promotions have become far larger than the actual revenue he makes from his other online businesses. It's not uncommon for Flynn to generate between $50,000 and $100,000 each month through his affiliate marketing efforts.

Rent Your Mailing List

If you have grown your mailing list to more than 25,000 subscribers, advertisers may be interested in paying you to send an email to your mailing list on their behalf on a cost-per-thousand (CPM) basis. If your mailing list is smaller than 25,000 subscribers, your list may not be large enough to attract the interest of advertisers yet. Let's say you have a mailing list of 30,000 subscribers, and an advertiser agrees to pay $40.00 CPM to email your list. They would pay you a total of $1,200 to send an email promoting their product or service. Renting your list to advertisers can be very profitable if you have built a large mailing list.

Finding Advertisers to Rent Your List

The biggest challenge with renting out your list is finding advertisers. Unless you are already established as a reputable mailing list owner with advertisers in your industry or are working with a reputable advertising agency that sells dedicated emails, you may have trouble letting advertisers know your list exists and is worth renting. There are disreputable publishers that try to sell mailings to low-quality, stolen, or scrapped mailing lists, so to avoid trouble advertisers primarily want to work with larger publishers that have built a good reputation.

If you are just getting started renting out your mailing list, your best bet is to find an advertising agency that works with mailing lists in your industry. You will be able to get a lot more list rentals if you can get a reputable agency to endorse and promote your mailing list. While an agency may take a 30%-50% commission on anything they sell, a *good* agency will make you far more than they cost you. Their sales team will be able to get you in front of advertisers that normally wouldn't talk to you and will even make deals on your behalf.

At MarketBeat, we currently work with a digital advertising agency out of Chicago called Investing Media Solutions. Investing Media Solutions sells newsletter sponsorships and dedicated emails through our mailing list to their advertisers in exchange for a percentage of each sale. They have been able to sell placements in our newsletter to advertisers that we could simply never make deals with directly, because they have existing relationships with some of the largest financial advertisers in the country. Investing Media Solutions handles all of the sales and billing work. MarketBeat just has to place the ads and collect checks at the end of each month. We generate between $15,000 and $25,000 each month through the newsletter sponsorships and dedicated emails that Investing Media Solutions sells on our behalf. We have had a great experience working with a digital advertising agency and believe it's definitely the way to go if you can find one of high quality.

The other option is to virtually pound the pavement and try to find advertisers by approaching them directly. You can identify advertisers by looking for them on your competitors' websites and mailing lists. If you are running Google AdSense ads on your website, you can see which advertisers are frequently showing up on your website and can approach them directly. You will need to put together a media kit which will highlight the size and demographic nature of your audience and will contain a list of various types of advertisements an advertiser can purchase. Approaching advertisers directly can be a lot of work but may be an effective way to generate list rental deals if you are a natural seller.

The Process of Renting Your List

When you make an agreement with an advertiser to rent your mailing list, there are several steps involved. You and the advertiser will agree to send an email to a set number of subscribers at a specific date and time. Several days before the email is scheduled to be sent, they will send you a copy of the email. You will then send a test email to the addresses they provide and will approve the message after they make sure everything looks right and the links are working properly. On the agreed upon day and time, you will send the email to your list. A few days after the email has been sent, the advertiser will generally request performance information about the send, such as total sends, total deliveries, total opens, and total clicks. You should provide that information to them in a timely manner. At the end of the month, you or your advertising agency will invoice them, and they will mail you a check 30 days later.

Run Co-Registration Advertising Units

In the list-building chapter of this book, we discussed co-registration advertising from the perspective of an advertiser. As a mailing list owner that collects organic opt-ins from your website, you can also generate revenue by running a co-registration advertising unit on the "thank you" page that subscribers see after signing up for your mailing list. After the user signs up for your mailing list, they will be presented with a list of additional offers they can also choose to opt in to. If a new subscriber selects any of the offers listed, you'll receive a small commission from the advertiser, and the subscriber's name and email address will automatically be passed on to the advertiser.

Co-registration advertising units can be wildly profitable if you receive a sizable number of opt-ins each month. On a normal page of your website, a display advertisement from Google AdSense or another network might yield between

$1.00 and $10.00 for every one thousand people that view the ad. A co-registration advertising unit can make anywhere from $200.00 to $750.00 for every thousand views on your "thank you" page. Users that have just opted in to your mailing list are extremely likely to engage with an advertisement, because they have already demonstrated they are willing to take action by signing up for your mailing list.

The amount of money you make from co-registration advertising will vary depending on the niche of your mailing list and the number of people that sign up for your email list on your website every month. Advertising networks that offer co-registration ads will often provide an estimate of what they believe your website can make for every new subscriber. For lower-value and general-interest mailing lists, you might be able to make an average of $0.15-$0.25 for every new subscriber that sees your co-registration advertising unit. For some specific niches, like finance and investing, publishers make between $0.60 and $1.00 for every subscriber that sees their co-registration advertising unit.

To calculate how much money a co-registration advertising unit could make your business in a given month, simply multiply the number of website opt-ins you get each month by the estimated amount of revenue you can make per view with your co-registration advertising unit.

While adding display ads to your website from a network like Google AdSense is a straightforward process, getting started with a company that offers co-registration advertising can be more involved. There are only a handful of advertising companies that offer co-registration advertising units, and you generally can't sign up for them by filling out a form on a website like you can with some networks. Typically, you will need to contact a number of co-registration advertising companies and provide them information about your mailing list and the demographics of your subscribers. They will give you an estimate of what they think you can make per impression with your mailing list and will typically want you to sign a 12-month agreement to run their unit. Placing ad code on your website for a co-registration unit is also a bit more involved than putting up a display ad, because you have to pass the subscriber's information back to the network through your ad tag. You can find a list of co-registration advertising companies in the list-building chapter of this book.

If you aren't collecting many opt-ins per month and co-registration advertising companies aren't interested in you, you can also monetize your "thank you" page with a display advertising unit from Google AdSense or another display advertising company. Your "thank you" page should be a relatively empty page with little more than a thank you message and the display ad centered on your page. While a "thank you" page with a display ad unit won't perform quite as well as a co-registration advertising unit, you will find that the ad unit on your "thank you" page can earn ten to fifteen times more than display ads on other pages.

At MarketBeat, we work with two different co-registration advertising companies, After Offers (afteroffers.com) and Investing Media Solutions (investingmediasolutions.com), to run co-registration advertising units on our "thank you" page. We also place co-registration ads on interstitial pages in front of special reports that we promote to our mailing list in order to generate additional ad revenue from these units. Through the networks we work with, we are able to generate between $20,000 and $30,000 monthly from the 20,000 organic opt-ins that we attract on a monthly basis.

Run Banner Ads in Your Newsletter

If you regularly publish a newsletter to your mailing list, there are advertising networks that will pay you to insert banner advertisements in your newsletter similar to those that might appear on your website. These ads are either sold on a cost-per-click (CPC) or cost-per-impression (CPM) basis. With these advertising networks, you will be given an HTML snippet to include in your newsletter. They will then sell ad placements in your newsletter to their network.

Here are some advertising networks that work with newsletter banner ads:

- **BuySellAds** – buysellads.com

- **LaunchBit** - launchbit.com

- **LiveIntent** – liveintent.com/platform

- **NewsletterDirectory.Co** - newsletterdirectory.co

Remember to keep a healthy balance between content and ads in your newsletter. The amount of educational and informative content should take up significantly more space than the ads. A good rule of thumb is to place an ad at the top of your newsletter and at the bottom of your newsletter, leaving the rest of the room for non-advertising content. If you have too many ads in your newsletter, subscribers will be less likely to engage with your content in the future.

At MarketBeat, we use a combination of text ads and banner ads in our daily newsletter. We work with an advertising network that sells text-based, cost-per-click advertisements in our newsletter to a number of different financial advertisers. The ads match the look and feel of the rest of our newsletter and are randomly rotated on a daily basis.

Drive Traffic to Your Website

If you have a website with a lot of content, chances are you are already running display advertisements from networks like Google AdSense, OpenX, Tribal Fusion, Taboola, and others. Whenever visitors come to your website and view and click on ads, you generate revenue—so the more visitors, the more money. Consider using your newsletter and other emails that you send as a traffic generation strategy for your website. If you can send your subscribers back to your website over and over again, they will likely view and click on more ads than they would otherwise.

Wrap-Up

While there are only a handful of different ways to monetize your mailing list, there are dozens of variations and twists on the six methods listed in this chapter. There are any number of ways to promote your own products and promote other companies' products as an affiliate to your list. Several co-registration advertising networks are available that you can run on your website, and a number of ways exist to generate revenue by including advertisements in your email content.

To get ideas for specific strategies to implement the six monetization methods listed in this chapter, learn from other mailing list owners that are already successfully monetizing their lists. Tim Bourquin, founder of AfterOffers.com, interviewed 42 different mailing list owners to see how they monetize their mailing lists in an epic blog post titled "42 Blogging Specialists Explain How to Monetize Email Newsletters and Turn Autoresponder Messages into Profit".[21]

Conclusion

- Run a special bonus or sale campaign to promote your company's products to your mailing list.

- Find two or three products that you can promote to your mailing list as an affiliate.

- Consider placing a co-registration advertising unit on your "thank you" page.

- Try to identify an advertising network that can place banners in your newsletter and help you rent your mailing list.

Chapter Seven

Email Deliverability and List Maintenance

When you send a letter through the U.S. mail with a stamp and a delivery address, you can be fairly certain your letter is going to arrive safely in a few days. This isn't always the case with email. While you shouldn't run into many issues if you are following the best practices and sending high-quality content to your mailing list, there's always the possibility of being added to a blacklist or facing some other deliverability issue that will prevent a percentage of the messages from being delivered or redirect them to subscribers' spam folders. For this reason, it's important to follow the best email practices and proactively monitor your mailing list for any issues that might hinder the deliverability of your messages.

Use an Email Service Provider (ESP)

To ensure every message possible makes it to the inboxes of your subscribers, you should always use an email service provider like MailChimp, Drip, or Aweber.

If you run your own mail server, you are likely to make configuration mistakes that will reduce your delivery rates. It would require finding your own mailing list software and actively monitoring the reputation of both your sending IP address (the Internet address that your email delivers from) and your domain name. Your ESP will handle all of the technical infrastructure and make sure you are following best practices to ensure your messages actually get to your subscribers' inboxes.

If you are paying less than $250.00 per month for your email service provider, know ahead of time that you might not be getting the best support in the world. ESPs make their real money from selling enterprise plans to large customers. They aren't always concerned with keeping people that have $25.00 or $50.00 per month plans happy with their services. You will typically receive the level of service that you pay for. If you are on a lower cost plan, know that you will need to take a more active role in monitoring and managing your email deliverability rates.

It can also be a good idea to have a backup email service provider in place. ESPs can shut your account off without notice if they believe you are spamming or if you inadvertently break another one of their rules. While this is a rare occurrence for most email service providers, it's always good to have a "Plan B" ready to go if your account gets blocked. Have a low-tier account set up with a second email service provider that allows you to import your mailing list from another provider. Finally, make sure you regularly backup your mailing list from your ESP, so you can move them to another provider if your account gets suspended.

Set Up DNS Verification Records

Email is a technology that was first developed in the 1970s. At the time, spam, viruses, and fraudulent emails weren't an issue. The technical specifications for email makes it very easy to fake the email address and domain name that sends any given email.

As the volume of spam and other fraudulent email has mushroomed, the Internet Engineering Task Force (IETF) has developed additional protocols that use your domain's DNS records to verify the origin of an email. The three major protocols include Sender Policy Framework (SPF), DomainKeys Identified Mail (DKIM), and Domain-based Message Authentication, Reporting, and Conformance (DMARC).

Internet service providers and other mail providers actively look for DNS entries that correspond to these email verification protocols. If your domain name does not have SPF and DKIM records set up, or if they are not set up properly, mail providers will often put your messages in your subscribers' spam folders. If they find other things wrong with your email or see that the IP address sending your email is on a blacklist, they may not deliver your messages at all.

You may or may not need to set up SPF records for your domain name depending on how your email service provider functions. Many ESPs will send email using one of their domains, which allows them to automatically add SPF, DKIM, and DMARC records without any intervention on your behalf. You will want to read your email service provider's documentation about them to determine whether or not you need to manually add SPF and DKIM to your DNS records.

If you are paying less than $100.00 per month, your ESP is probably sending mail using one of their domain names on your behalf. If you are using a high-end plan and your ESP supports what's known as white labeling, you may need to add SPF and DKIM records to your domain's DNS records.

Here are some domain authentication guides put together by major ESPs. Read the guide associated with your email service provider to get the information most relevant to you:

- AWeber - help.aweber.com/hc/en-us/articles/204026716-What-s-Email-Authentication-How-Does-It-Apply-To-Me-

- Campaign Monitor - help.campaignmonitor.com/topic.aspx?t=88

- Constant Contact - support2.constantcontact.com/articles/FAQ/1556

- Drip - getdrip.com/faq

- ExactTarget - help.exacttarget.com/en-US/documentation/exacttarget/resources/sender_policy_framework/

- GetResponse - support.getresponse.com/uploads/2011/09/9048Dd01.pdf

- iContact - icontact.com/static/pdf/Email_Marketing_Best_Practic es_iContact.pdf

- MailChimp - kb.mailchimp.com/delivery/deliverability- research/set-up-mailchimp-authentication

- SendGrid - sendgrid.com/docs/Glossary/spf.html

SPF Records

Sender Policy Framework, better known as SPF, is an email validation technology that detects mail spoofing by allowing ISPs and other email services to verify whether or not any given email from a domain name has been authorized by the administrators of that domain. A domain owner will publish a list of IP addresses and other domains authorized to send mail on their behalf as a specially-formatted text DNS record. Whenever a mail server receives an incoming message, they can use a domain's SPF records to verify that the email was sent by a server with permission to send email on behalf of that domain.

If your email service provider sends out mail using its own domain, you don't have to worry about setting up SPF records. If your email service provider sends out mail using your domain name or supports white labeling, then setting up appropriate SPF records for your domain is mandatory.

While there's a lot of technical jargon surrounding SPF and other DNS verification tools, setting them up isn't all that difficult. For example, I use SendGrid as my primary email service provider. In order to tell the world that SendGrid has permission to email on behalf of my domain name, I would need to use "v=spf1 include:sendgrid.net ~all" as the text in my SPF record. The "include:sendgrid.net" indicates that SendGrid can send email on my behalf and the "~all" indicates that other sources claiming to be sending mail on behalf of my domain may not be trustworthy.

To find the appropriate SPF record for your email service provider, simply do a web search for the name of your email service provider followed by "SPF." Once you have identified the appropriate record, you will need to log in to your domain name registrar and add the appropriate record.

Many email service providers will walk you through this process as part of your initial setup with specific instructions and step-by-step guides. If that's not the case, there are dozens of videos on YouTube which will show you how to add SPF records to your domain. You can use a tool published by MX Toolbox to verify the placement of your SPF records, which is located at mxtoolbox.com/spf.aspx.

DKIM Records

DomainKeys Identified Mail (DKIM) is another email validation technology that verifies a sender has permission from a domain's administrators to send email on behalf of a particular domain. Additionally, DKIM allows messages to be individually signed using public key encryption so a recipient mail server can verify a message has not been modified during transport. Any DKIM enabled email will include a digital signature that an email server can use, along with a domain's public DKIM encryption key to ensure the message received is identical to the message that was originally sent. Like SPF records, DKIM records are placed in a domain's DNS records. Most major email service providers sign their outgoing mail with DKIM, including Gmail, Outlook.com, Yahoo, and AOL.

If your email service provider uses its own domain name to send mail on your behalf, DKIM keys will already be set up without any work on your part. If your email service provider sends mail using your domain (sometimes known as white labeling), you should set up DKIM records in your domain's DNS records to maximize deliverability rates. Unlike SPF records, which are usually the same for every user of an email service provider, DKIM keys must be generated on a per domain basis. You will need to acquire DKIM DNS records directly from your email service provider and copy them into your DNS records. You can use a separate tool published by MX Toolbox to verify the placement of DKIM records, which is located at mxtoolbox.com/dkim.aspx.

DMARC Records

Domain-based Message Authentication, Reporting, and Conformance (DMARC) is a newer protocol that builds upon the DKIM and SPF records used to detect mail spoofing. Placing a DMARC record in your domain tells mail providers that your domain is protected by SPF and DKIM authentications. DMARC records also provide instructions to mail servers relating to how messages that can't be properly authenticated should be handled. A domain owner can use a DMARC record to instruct mail service providers to either put messages that fail authentication into a user's junk mail folder or not deliver them at all.

In most cases, it's probably not necessary to add DMARC records to your domain. While SPF and DKIM records validate that an email comes from your domain name, DMARC merely provides instructions regarding what to do with messages that can't be authenticated. They probably won't positively impact your email deliverability, and can also cause legitimate email to be rejected if they are not set up properly.

Single Opt-In vs. Double Opt-In

When a subscriber first signs up for your mailing list, you may or may not require the subscriber to click on a link in a confirmation email to confirm their subscription. A mailing list that requires a subscriber to click through on a confirmation is known as a "double opt-in" mailing list, because users first opt-in on your website and then opt-in again through the link in your confirmation email. Mailing lists that simply add new users to its subscriber list without sending a confirmation email are known as single opt-ins.

Some email service providers (ESPs) require their customers to operate double opt-in mailing lists and will not add a new subscriber to your mailing list unless they click a link in a confirmation email. Other ESPs are more flexible and allow you to choose between requiring a single opt-in or a double opt-in. If your ESP requires a double opt-in, you don't have much of a say in the matter. If you have a more flexible ESP, you will have to decide whether a single opt-in is sufficient or if you want to require a double opt-in.

For many years, requiring a double opt-in was seen as a best practice for email marketers. By requiring a double opt-in, you know that every subscriber signing up for your mailing list actually wants to receive messages from you, because they have to click a link in a confirmation email that's specific to their email account to verify they want your messages.

Statistics show that confirmed opt-in mailing lists receive better than average open rates, fewer bounces, and fewer issues with deliverability, primarily because bad email addresses don't get added to double opt-in mailing lists.[22]

With a single opt-in mailing list, a bad actor can easily subscribe other people to your mailing list by entering their email addresses into your opt-in forms. It's also possible that people are inadvertently added to mailing lists when a new subscriber accidentally enters a typo into an opt-in form. While these inadvertent opt-ins are pretty rare, they have been used as a reason for some ESPs to require mailing list operators to use double opt-ins.

During the last few years, the tide has been shifting among marketers to favor only requiring a single opt-in. Single opt-in proponents argue that it's not in the best interest of marketers to make it harder for subscribers to sign up for their mailing lists. Opt-in confirmation rates have been falling during the last few years, which has led double opt-in mailing list operators to wonder if they are losing subscribers that would otherwise be engaged and interested in their content.

Single opt-in mailing lists generally grow much faster than double opt-in mailing lists. While they might have lower open rates and higher bounce rates, single opt-in mailing lists tend to have a higher total number of engaged subscribers.

For more information about why marketers are moving away from requiring double opt-ins, read the blog post, "Double Opt-In Is Destroying Your List and Your Business"[23] on the AfterOffers blog.

At MarketBeat, we do not require a double opt-in. We believe we would lose too many subscribers before they have a chance to decide if they like our content. Instead, we include a very prominent opt-out link in our welcome email and use data provided by our email service provider to automatically remove invalid and spam-reporting email addresses from our mailing list.

We also use engagement metrics to automatically remove inactive subscribers. If we can't confirm that a user has opened an email from us within the last six months, we remove them from our mailing list. Even though we don't require a double opt-in, we maintain an average deliverability rate of 99.5% and an average open rate of 21%, because we automatically clear out invalid and inactive email addresses from our mailing list.

User Engagement Matters

Major email providers, including Gmail, Outlook, Yahoo, and AOL, are increasingly focusing on how users are engaging with your messages to determine whether or not your messages will appear in your subscribers' inboxes or their junk mail folders. If a user opens an email, replies to an email, or clicks on a link in an email, an ISP knows that the user is engaged with the message and probably wanted to receive it. If a subscriber regularly deletes or simply ignores an email, it's probably a spam message or another email that a subscriber didn't want to receive.

Email providers will look at the aggregate engagement data of all of their subscribers over time to determine the quality and relevance of email sent by a given domain name and IP address.

For example, if you send an email to 1,000 people at a particular ISP and only five of them actually open your message, the ISP is likely to believe their users probably don't want your email and may put future emails that you send in their users' spam folders. On the other hand, if you send an email to 1,000 people at an ISP and 400 of them open the message and click on a link in the email, the ISP will know that their users are engaged with your content and that future messages you send should be placed in their users' inboxes.

In order to maximize your deliverability rates over time, you will want to try and write email in such a way that encourages users to be engaged with your content as measured by the metrics that mail providers use to track engagement--opens, clicks, and replies. Use engaging subject lines to persuade users to open your email. Include several links in each email with a clear call-to-action.

Most importantly, try to get users to periodically reply to your messages. You can do this by asking your subscribers for their feedback and having them provide their answers by replying to your messages.

You should also actively remove invalid, inactive, and spam-reporting email addresses from your mailing list in order to keep your engagement rates high. Remove users that report *your* messages as spam from your mailing list. They probably don't want to receive your messages, and receiving too many spam reports can jeopardize your relationship with your email service provider.

If a subscriber's email address gets returned as invalid (sometimes referred to as a hard bounce), you should remove their email address from your mailing list, because they are never going to receive your message regardless of how many times you try.

Finally, you should remove any subscriber from your mailing list that has not opened any of your messages within the last 12 months. Having extremely inactive subscribers on your mailing list will hurt your average engagement rates. Plus, it is not worth paying your email service provider to email subscribers that are never going to open your messages.

Your ESP's Role in Deliverability

The level of assistance your email service provider will offer regarding deliverability is generally proportional to the monthly fee that you are paying. As an enterprise customer of SendGrid, my dedicated sending IP addresses and my domains are automatically checked against blacklists on a daily basis. If they see any issues, they will automatically file a removal request on my behalf.

I have a dedicated account representative that can personally intervene with any issues I have, and I will also receive email notifications if my deliverability rate drops below a certain percentage so I can take remedial action. While having additional delivery monitoring and blacklist remediation services are nice, they are usually only available to very high-end customers that send hundreds of thousands of messages each month. If you are paying

$25.00-$50.00 per month to your email service provider, you will need to take a more proactive role in the deliverability of your email by regularly monitoring your deliverability rates and checking for blacklist issues.

Check for Reputation, Blacklist, and Deliverability Issues

The most important thing that you can do to ensure your emails continue to make it into your subscribers' inboxes over the long term is proactively monitor for issues on a regular basis. Your domain name or the IP address that sends your email can be added to a blacklist at any date and time without any kind of notice. For this reason, it's important to set up a weekly or bi-weekly plan to verify that your messages are getting properly delivered to your subscribers' inboxes.

Here are the recommended steps you should follow each week to monitor your deliverability rates:

- **Review Statistics Provided by Your ESP** – Your email service provider will generate delivery statistics for each email that you send. Review the statistics for all of the emails you sent in the last week. If your average bounce rate increases by one percent or more, or if your average delivery rates fall by one percent or more, your domain or sending IP address may have been added to a blacklist.

- **Use MultiRBL to Check for Blacklist Issues** – MultiRBL (multirbl.valli.org) can check your domain name or the IP address that sends your email against 224 known blacklists. There are several other online tools that check for blacklists, but MultiRBL is by far the most comprehensive. If your ISP has assigned you a dedicated IP address, you will need to check both your domain name and the IP address assigned by your ESP for delivery issues. If you don't have a dedicated IP address, you will only need to check your domain name against MultiRBL, because your ESP will automatically monitor their shared IP addresses for blacklist issues. Note that smaller ESP service plans generally do not include a dedicated IP address.

- **Review Your Recent Bounced Messages** – Your ESP should provide a log of recent bounced messages, along with a message from the recipient's email server as to why the message couldn't be properly delivered. You should scan through this list every week to identify any potential blacklist issues. If you see a similar error message appear several times in a row, you should take the time to identify and address the issue. If you find that your delivery rates are dropping, your bounced messages log will usually help you identify the root cause.

- **Check Your Sender Score (Optional)** – SenderScore (senderscore.org) compiles a massive amount of email data from ISPs and other mail providers. Their free reporting tool can warn you about a number of deliverability issues relating to your sending IP address, such as spam reports, blacklists, and spam traps. If you haven't received a dedicated IP address from your email service provider, you can skip this step.

- **Check for Email Provider Specific Issues (Optional)**
  – Consider creating a new account with Gmail,
  Outlook.com, Yahoo, and AOL for the sole purpose of
  subscribing to your mailing list to see if any messages
  show up in your spam folder. If you regularly see
  messages sent to a certain email provider showing up
  in a spam folder, you probably have a deliverability
  issue that needs to be addressed. If you want to
  automate this process, you can use a service called
  MailMonitor (mailmonitorapp.com), which will tell
  you whether or not you have any deliverability issues
  with specific ISPs and email providers. At $79.00 per
  month, MailMonitor is probably only worth paying
  for if you have a list of 25,000 subscribers or more.

Place a recurring note in your calendar on the same day
every week to check for deliverability issues. The process
only takes five minutes but can be easy to forget if you don't
set a calendar reminder.

What to Do When You Get Blacklisted

If you have a large mailing list, you are inevitably going to
land on a blacklist at some point. There are hundreds of
blacklists maintained on the web, and each has its own
specific set of guidelines that can cause your domain name
or sending IP address to be blacklisted. Invariably, too many
users will click a "report spam" button, or you will send too
many bounced messages and your domain or IP will get
added to a blacklist. When this happens, don't let it ruin
your day. Most blacklists are only used by a very small
number of email services, and it's usually pretty easy to get
yourself removed from blacklists.

In order to get yourself removed from a blacklist, you typically need to complete a short form on the blacklist operator's website. You can usually find the link to the removal form in your log of recent bounced messages or through MultiRBL's blacklist scanner.

If you can't find the link to the removal form or can't seem to get yourself removed from a blacklist, email your service provider's support address and ask for help. Sometimes, an ESP can get your domain or sending IP address removed from a blacklist when you cannot get the job done yourself.

Reduce Spam Complaints

Most ISPs and other mail providers include a "report spam" link that allows their users to mark an email as spam. When a user clicks that button, the message will be moved into the user's spam folder, and your ESP will be notified of the spam complaint.

Your email service provider will want you to maintain a spam complaint rate of less than 0.1%. That means for every 10,000 emails you send, you should receive at most 10 spam complaints. If your complaint rate is consistently higher than 0.1%, your email service provider may intervene and shut down your account, or ask you to make changes to your sending practices and reduce the high complaint rate.

In order to keep your complaint rate below 0.1%, you should make the process to unsubscribe from your mailing list as easy as possible. Make sure there is a link to unsubscribe from your mailing list in every email and that the link works properly.

If your complaint rate is high, you can reduce the number of spam complaints you receive by placing an unsubscribe link in both the header and the footer of your email.

If supported by your email service provider, add an unsubscribe header which will allow email providers to add their own unsubscribe button near the "Report Spam" button. An unsubscribe header is a hidden field in an email that provides technical instructions relating to how a subscriber can request to be removed from your mailing list. Using an unsubscribe header is quickly becoming a best practice and can help you avoid many spam complaints. To learn how to implement an unsubscribe header, visit list-unsubscribe.com.

Check Outgoing Emails for Issues

Whenever you are getting ready to send a broadcast email to your mailing list, you should check the message for any potential issues by using your email service provider's spam check tool. If your ESP does not provide a spam checking tool, there are a number of free services including Mail Tester (mailtester.com) and Contactology's Spam Checker (info.contactology.com/check-mqs). These tools will serve as an early warning system and let you know if any questionable content or formatting exists in your messages that are likely to set off a spam filter.

For example, messages that promise users they can make a lot of money or messages that reference erectile dysfunction medications are almost always spam. Spam filters know this and will filter them out accordingly. If you inadvertently put too many dollar signs in your email or make a joke about

Viagra, spam checking tools will warn you that the content in your email may be an issue before you press the send button.

Schedule Your Messages for Optimal Engagement

When sending a broadcast email message to your audience, you may be naturally inclined to send it immediately after you finish writing it regardless of the time or day. However, there are specific days of the week and times of day that you can send a message in order to maximize the number of people that see and open them.

Many email marketers believe that Tuesdays, Wednesdays, and Thursdays are the best days of the week to send email. Your subscribers are generally at work on those days and will be actively checking their email. During the weekend, they are less likely to be at their computers and are less likely to open messages. If you send an email on a Saturday morning and a subscriber doesn't check their messages until Monday morning, your message may be buried below 100 other received emails.

You will want to do your own testing to verify which days of the week work best for your mailing list. I have personally had great engagement rates by sending email on Saturday and Sunday mornings, when subscribers aren't receiving much other marketing email.

If possible, try to send your messages at the beginning of the work day (around 8:00 AM) or toward the end of the work day (around 4:00 PM) when your subscribers are more likely to be checking their email. If supported by your ESP, segment your mailing list by time zone, so that your subscribers will receive your message at 8:00 AM or 4:00 PM in their local time. At MarketBeat, we don't have the capability to segment by time zone. We generally send messages at 9:00 AM Eastern Time, so most of the United States will receive our messages at or near the beginning of the work day.

Dealing with Gmail's Multiple Inboxes

In 2014, Gmail began separating its user's inboxes into three separate tabs. In addition to a user's primary inbox, messages from social networking sites are getting put into their own tab, and messages that Gmail considers to be marketing material are sent into a tab called "Promotions."

Because users don't see emails that are put into the promotions tab by default, some email marketers have noticed that their open rates among Gmail users have declined significantly after this change was rolled out. Some email marketers have panicked over this change because they fear they are going to lose sales due to lower open rates and because they believe their messages are unfairly landing in the promotions tab. While Gmail's multiple tabs are a concern for email marketers, there are a couple of proven ways that marketers can get their messages back in user's primary inboxes. The first thing that you can do is send an email to your Gmail subscribers and ask them to drag your message from the "promotions" tab to the "primary" tab, so they won't miss out on any of the great content you plan on sending them. You might also want to include a quick YouTube video that shows people how to do this to make the process dead simple.

The second thing that you can do to get back in your subscribers' "primary" tab is to get them to reply to your messages. If a subscriber replies to your messages, Gmail will be more likely to believe your messages are important and will put them in the subscriber's "primary" tab. The best time to ask users for a reply is in your welcome message. Simply include a short message like, "Could you reply to this message to let me know that you've received it? I want to make sure that there aren't any issues with your subscription," in your first welcome email. While not everyone will reply, many will.

Gmail and other email providers will continue to develop their email interfaces over time. Don't panic when a major email service provider changes how email is presented to their subscribers. Marketers always find ways to adapt to new features and interface changes that email providers introduce.

Wrap-Up

While it can be easy to feel overwhelmed by the technical components of email deliverability, you don't have to become an expert overnight.

Many deliverability issues won't surface until you have built a large subscriber list and you begin to send a lot of email. Follow the basic monitoring recommendations outlined in this chapter, and you'll know right away if there's a problem that needs to be addressed.

There are a number of resources available, such as SendGrid's Deliverability Guide[24], which can help you learn about the intricacies of email deliverability and help you solve any deliverability issues you run into. If you can't figure out how to fix a deliverability issue on your own, your ESP can always step in to help, too.

Action Steps

- Use an email service provider to send out every message to your mailing list.

- Set up appropriate SPF, DKIM, and DMARC records if required by your ESP.

- Decide whether or not you want to require a single opt-in or a double opt-in.

- Create a weekly or bi-weekly calendar reminder to check for deliverability issues.

- Use Mail Tester or another tool to check for potential issues before sending broadcast emails to your mailing list.

Chapter Eight

Legal Aspects of Email Marketing

While email marketing and other aspects of Internet businesses can sometimes feel like you are operating in the Wild West, email marketing is actually regulated in the United States, Canada, and in some other developed countries. You will want to learn about your country's specific regulations regarding email marketing, so you can stay in compliance with the law and avoid getting hit with hefty penalties for unknowingly committing violations.

CAN-SPAM Act of 2003 (United States)

Congress passed the Controlling the Assault of Non-Solicited Pornography And Marketing Act in 2003, better known as the CAN-SPAM Act. CAN-SPAM establishes a basic set of rules for all commercial email. Each separate violation of the CAN-SPAM Act can result in penalties of up to $16,000, so it's important to make sure your messages stay compliant with the law.

The Federal Trade Commission has put together a guide for businesses titled "CAN-SPAM Act: A Compliance Guide for Business," which is located at 1.usa.gov/1wftWeD.

The guide outlines the main requirements of CAN-SPAM and provides a series of frequently asked questions that clarify different components of the legislation.

I recommend every mailing list owner in the United States read this guide.

Here are some of the main requirements of CAN-SPAM listed in the guide:

1. **Don't use false or misleading header information.**
   Your "From," "To," "Reply-To," and routing information—including the originating domain name and email address—must be accurate and identify the person or business who initiated the message.

2. **Don't use deceptive subject lines.**
   The subject line must accurately reflect the content of the message.

3. **Identify the message as an ad.**
   The law gives you a lot of leeway in how to do this, but you must disclose clearly and conspicuously that your message is an advertisement.

4. **Tell recipients where you're located.**
   Your message must include your valid physical postal address. This can be your current street address, a post office box you've registered with the U.S. Postal Service, or a private mailbox you've

registered with a commercial mail receiving agency established under Postal Service regulations.

5. **Tell recipients how to opt out of receiving future email from you.**
   Your message must include a clear and conspicuous explanation of how the recipient can opt out of getting email from you in the future. Craft the notice in a way that's easy for an ordinary person to recognize, read, and understand. Creative use of type size, color, and location can improve clarity. Give a return email address or another easy Internet-based way to allow people to communicate their choice to you. You may create a menu to allow a recipient to opt out of certain types of messages, but you must include the option to stop all commercial messages from you. Make sure your spam filter doesn't block these opt-out requests.

6. **Honor opt-out requests promptly.**
   Any opt-out mechanism you offer must be able to process opt-out requests for at least 30 days after you send your message. You must honor a recipient's opt-out request within 10 business days. You can't charge a fee, require the recipient to give you any personal identifying information beyond an email address, or make the recipient take any step other than sending a reply email or visiting a single page on an Internet website as a condition for honoring an opt-out request. Once people have told you they don't want to receive more messages from you, you can't sell or transfer their email addresses, even in the form of a mailing list. The only exception is that you

may transfer the addresses to a company you've hired to help you comply with the CAN-SPAM Act.

7. **Monitor what others are doing on your behalf.** The law makes clear that even if you hire another company to handle your email marketing, you can't contract away your legal responsibility to comply with the law. Both the company whose product is promoted in the message and the company that actually sends the message may be held legally responsible.

There have been a number of criminal indictments under the CAN-SPAM Act of 2003 since its passage. To date, only a handful of large-scale spam operations have been targeted by the Federal Trade Commission.

Most small marketers probably don't need to worry much about the FTC knocking on their door over a violation, but you should still ensure your mailings are in compliance with the CAN-SPAM Act. The rules outlined by the Federal Trade Commission are straightforward and are very easy to follow. Be honest about who you are, where your business is located, and the content of your messages. Provide clear opt-out instructions and honor opt-out request promptly. Do these two things, and you probably won't have much to worry about.

Interestingly enough, the CAN-SPAM Act of 2003 doesn't actually outlaw spam. The legislation does not require commercial email senders to get permission before emailing someone. When the legislation was first passed, some referred to it as the "You Can Spam" Act, because it didn't actually do anything to limit the amount of spam that people receive.

The CAN-SPAM Act also generally only applies to people living in the United States. Many spammers are located in developing countries around the globe, which makes it extremely difficult to take any legal action against them. Because of the limited jurisdiction of the CAN-SPAM Act and its relatively light regulatory burden, spam continues to be a major problem in the United States and the rest of the world.

FTC Endorsement Guidelines (United States)

If you are going to promote another company's products as an affiliate, you need to be aware of the Federal Trade Commission's paid endorsement guidelines. Generally, you need to disclose whenever you are getting paid to promote a product or service for another company. Your disclosure must also be "clear and conspicuous" and as close to the endorsement as possible. This means that you shouldn't try to hide your disclosure in the footer of your messages or in some other inconspicuous location.

The Federal Trade Commission issued a guide in March 2013 that outlines disclosure rules and recommendations for paid digital media endorsements titled, ".com Disclosures: How to Make Effective Disclosures in Digital Advertising".[25]

Here's a great example email from marketer Pat Flynn about how to properly disclose affiliate relationships in an email:

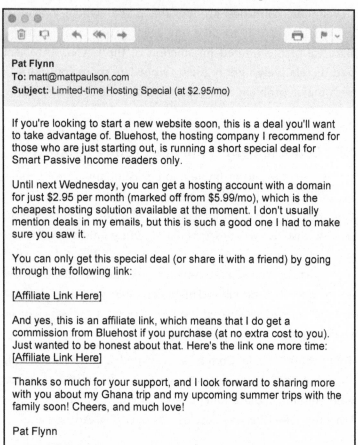

Pat Flynn
To: matt@mattpaulson.com
Subject: Limited-time Hosting Special (at $2.95/mo)

If you're looking to start a new website soon, this is a deal you'll want to take advantage of. Bluehost, the hosting company I recommend for those who are just starting out, is running a short special deal for Smart Passive Income readers only.

Until next Wednesday, you can get a hosting account with a domain for just $2.95 per month (marked off from $5.99/mo), which is the cheapest hosting solution available at the moment. I don't usually mention deals in my emails, but this is such a good one I had to make sure you saw it.

You can only get this special deal (or share it with a friend) by going through the following link:

[Affiliate Link Here]

And yes, this is an affiliate link, which means that I do get a commission from Bluehost if you purchase (at no extra cost to you). Just wanted to be honest about that. Here's the link one more time: [Affiliate Link Here]

Thanks so much for your support, and I look forward to sharing more with you about my Ghana trip and my upcoming summer trips with the family soon! Cheers, and much love!

Pat Flynn

Canada's Anti-Spam Legislation (CASL)

The Canadian Parliament passed the Fighting Internet and Wireless Spam Act (FISA) in December 2010. The legislation, better known by the nickname of Canada's Anti-Spam Legislation (CASL), went into effect on July 1st, 2014. CASL requires that marketers only send email to individuals who consent to receive messages, with a few exceptions. CASL is arguably one of the most stringent pieces of anti-spam legislation in the world due to its consent requirements and other restrictions put in place by the legislation.

Under CASL, you can only send email to subscribers that have expressly opted in to your mailing list or to recipients that have passively agreed to accept email through some form of implied consent.

For example, you can email anyone that's purchased a product from you or has done a business deal with you within the last 24 months under the guise of implied consent. There are also a variety of exceptions for recipients that you have an existing personal or business relationship with and for recipients that you need to notify of a product recall, court order, or updates and changes to an existing product or service they previously purchased.

CASL also puts a number of other restrictions on marketers. The legislation requires mailing list operators to have a working opt-out mechanism. CASL also makes it illegal to harvest email addresses using software and installing computer programs without consent. The legislation makes it illegal to alter messages in transit *and* makes it illegal to use false or misleading representations online in the promotion of products or services.

The legislation is enforced by the Canadian Competition Bureau, the Canadian Office of the Privacy Commissioner, and the Canadian Radio-television and Telecommunications Commission (CRTC). Individuals that violate the legislation can face fines of up to one million dollars, and businesses in

206 | Email Marketing Demystified

violation can face fines of up to $10 million. The law will go into full effect in 2017 when private citizens can take civil action against spammers that violate the provisions of CASL.

If you don't live in Canada, you might think that the provisions of CASL won't apply to you. However, if you live in the United States or another jurisdiction and have subscribers in Canada, you need to pay attention to the legislation.

CASL applies where "a computer system located in Canada is used to send or access" an electronic message.[26] This means that CASL will apply if a sender in the United States sends an email to a Canadian citizen who opens it on a computer or smartphone located in Canada.

While it remains to be seen if Canada will try to enforce the CASL outside of its borders through extradition, it's probably a good idea to stay in compliance with CASL if you are going to have any Canadian customers.

The American Bar Association has published an article that contains additional information about CASL's implications for citizens in other countries titled "Canada's Tough New Anti-Spam Legislation: Beware Its Extra-Territorial Reach".[27]

For more information about CASL and how to stay compliant, visit fightspam.gc.ca.

Wrap-Up

While regulations that surround email marketing will vary depending on what country you live in, you probably won't have a lot to worry about if you follow what I refer to as the *three golden rules of email marketing*:

1. Only send email to people that have opted in to receiving your messages.

2. Only send content that you would actually want to receive if you were a subscriber to your mailing list.

3. Don't be deceptive in the content of your messages, and don't try to hide your identity to your subscribers.

If you only send high-quality, relevant, and honest content to your subscribers and you only email people that have expressly opted in to your mailing list, it's extremely unlikely that anyone is ever going to get upset with you enough to try to hit you over the head with a civil suit for failing to follow anti-spam legislation. You should still pay attention to your country's anti-spam legislation and try to follow its provisions, but you won't have a target on your back if you follow the three golden rules of email marketing.

Action Steps

- If you live in the United States, verify that your email sending practices are in compliance with the CAN-SPAM Act of 2003.

- If you live in Canada, verify that your email sending practices are in compliance with Canada's Anti-Spam Legislation (CASL).

- If you live in another country, research your own country's anti-spam laws to make sure you are in compliance with your country's laws and regulations.

- Follow the three golden rules of email marketing.

Chapter Nine

Outbound Email Marketing

The majority of this book has focused on using email as a means of building an engaged audience and generating revenue by selling or recommending products to that audience. While growing a community surrounding your content can work well in many categories, it isn't ideal in others. You can easily build a mailing list in niches that cater to hobbyists and general consumers, but it's much more difficult to grow a mailing list if your company sells a very specific product to certain types of people or businesses. If your company makes a very niche product with a relatively high price point and only has a few thousand potential customers, you are much better off approaching your prospective customers on a one-on-one basis rather than doing traditional list building and trying to attract an audience.

For example, if I ran a farm implement dealer that sold tractors, balers, and combines to local farmers, there might only be a few hundred farms that would ever purchase equipment from my business. My potential customer base simply would not be large enough for building a subscriber list outside of my existing customer base to be worthwhile. This doesn't mean email marketing isn't a valid marketing strategy for this business, but it *does* mean I would need to take a different approach.

I would still send email with news and product information to my current customers, but that wouldn't be my only email marketing efforts. Instead of waiting for local farmers to sign up to receive email from me, I would need to use email as an outreach tool and try to schedule appointments with farmers or invite them into my dealership.

This marketing strategy, known as email prospecting, involves sending personal email messages to certain members of specific organizations in hopes of accomplishing a specific sales objective. When you send a prospecting email, the prospective customers that receive the message won't have opted into your mailing list and generally won't know who you are prior to receiving your email.

At my fictional implement dealer, I might try to get referrals from some of my existing customers. I would then send a cold email to the referral and ask if there is any equipment they plan on buying in the next 12-24 months, and show them what the dealership has that might be able to meet their needs.

Email prospecting won't necessarily replace the need to collect opt-ins on your website, build an email list, and send a mix of content and marketing material to your subscribers in hopes of generating sales. Even large B2B companies with extremely high price points publish white papers that require a reader to opt in to their mailing list before getting access to the white paper.

Think of email prospecting as a complement to your existing list-building efforts. While traditional autoresponder messages and broadcast emails will engage subscribers that complete opt-in forms on your website, email prospecting will engage potential customers that have never heard of you or your business. Both work together in a complementary manner to generate new business for your company.

Inbound Marketing vs. Outbound Marketing

Inbound marketing refers to marketing activities that draw customers into your business by creating compelling content and earning your potential customer's attention. Gathering opt-ins and sending autoresponders and broadcast emails to your mailing list are both inbound marketing techniques. Outbound marketing techniques involve actively identifying potential customers through list gathering, social networks, and going out and getting their attention. Cold calling, cold emailing, running commercials, placing advertisements, and attending trade shows are examples of outbound marketing techniques. The remainder of this chapter will focus on outbound email marketing, also known as email prospecting. Email prospecting is the process of identifying potential customers for your company's products or services and sending them a cold email in hopes of getting their attention.

Isn't Email Prospecting Considered Spamming?

Throughout the first several chapters of the book, I recommended that you only email people that have expressly opted in to your mailing list. However, I also suggest that sending a cold email introducing yourself to prospects can be an effective marketing strategy if you run a certain type of business. These two statements can seem somewhat contradictory at face value, but sending someone a personalized cold email introducing yourself is very different than spamming them.

Spamming occurs when a marketer sends a large volume of unwanted commercial email over a period of time. Sending one or two targeted message to a specific person at a business for a specific reason is not spamming. It's the difference between sending a few people a single, personal letter and incessantly sending 5,000 people mail they don't want. Sending cold emails for business development purposes is a generally accepted practice in most industries.

Identifying Potential Customers

Amidst your inbound email marketing efforts, potential customers will self-identify themselves by signing up for your mailing list. When doing outbound email marketing, you will need to go out and identify potential customers that you can approach.

You probably already know what types of people or businesses are your potential customers. You just need to find the specific prospects that meet your criteria.

There are several ways that you can identify potential customers:

- **LinkedIn** – LinkedIn has become an increasingly popular way for salespeople to identify potential customers. A user's LinkedIn profile will provide detailed information about their career and personal interests, which makes it a perfect tool to find potential customers. LinkedIn has advanced search tools that let you hone in on specific types of people easily. While it is a great way to identify potential customers, you shouldn't use LinkedIn to contact your potential customers, because many users don't check their LinkedIn messages. Your message may then get lost among the many less-targeted marketing messages that subscribers receive.

- **Facebook Fan Pages** – Identify Facebook fan pages that are relevant to your potential customers. People will frequently self-identify as needing help to solve a particular problem by posting to that fan page's wall and asking for suggestions. If you see someone that has written about a problem that your business can solve, send them a message through Facebook to introduce yourself and tell them how that you can help them.

- **Twitter Search** – People will also frequently self-identify problems they need help with by tweeting about them. For example, if you are a web designer, you might do a Twitter search for a phrase like "recommend a web designer" to find people who are looking to hire a web designer. On the date that I wrote this chapter, ten people have specifically asked if anyone can recommend a web designer to them within the last week. Search for multiple phrases people might use to indicate they have a problem you can solve. Once you identify a potential customer, tweet them, and you might be able to help with their problem. Try to get their email address, so you can send them an introduction email or their phone number to setup a call.

- **Lead Scoring** – If you have an existing mailing list, you can use a process known as lead scoring to identify the subscribers most likely to become your customers. Lead scoring is simply the process of calculating an engagement score for your subscribers based on the actions that they take, such as reading emails, clicking on links, requesting free reports, following you on social media, etc. If someone is highly engaged with your content, they will be much more likely to become a customer of your business. By calculating a lead score for each of your subscribers, you can see which of your potential subscribers you should put the most time and effort into to acquire them as a customer.

- **Compile a List** – Consider hiring a virtual assistant, an intern, or a relatively low-cost employee to help identify businesses and people that meet your criteria. Have them collect all of the key information you would need to send a cold email and put it in a spreadsheet, including the name of the business, the location, the owner, the business's phone number, and the owner's email address. For example, if you wanted to create a list of chiropractors, you could have an intern do a web search for chiropractors in specific cities in the geographic region you are targeting and add them to your spreadsheet. A list that you compile yourself will generally be more up-to-date and accurate than a list you purchase from a list broker.

- **Trade Shows** – Consider getting a booth at the trade shows that are frequented by your potential customers. While your first thought might be to get a booth at an industry trade show, remember that industry trade shows generally cater to people that *work* in an industry and not customers that buy products from that industry. If you were a chiropractor, you would want to get a booth at a trade show frequented by people that have back pain and not an industry show for other chiropractors. While at a show, collect as many business cards as possible, so you can follow up with potential leads via email after the show.

- **Ask for Referrals** – Whenever you get a new customer, ask them whether or not they can recommend anyone else that might benefit from your company's products or services. By getting referrals from your existing customers, you've instantly identified a new warm lead that you can follow up on.

Finding a Potential Customer's Email Address

When you identify a customer through social media channels such as Twitter, Facebook, and LinkedIn, their email address may not be listed on their social media profile. In some cases, you can get a potential customer's email address just by asking them. If this isn't the case, you will need to do some sleuthing on the web to identify a person's email address, so you can send them an introduction letter.

Here are some ways to find a potential customer's email address:

- **Google Them** – Google the name of your potential customer and the name of their business (if applicable). You may find other websites or other social media profiles that a person has created that do contain their email address. Make sure you go through the first several pages of search results in order to find all potential websites that may contain pertinent contact information. For more targeted results, consider doing a search of their company's domain name. For example, you could search "site:marketbeat.com Matthew Paulson" to find references to me on my company's website.

- **Make an Educated Guess** – Most companies use a standardized format for their email addresses. For example, all Bank of America employees' email addresses are in the format of firstname.lastname@bankofamerica.com. If I were a Bank of America employee and you were trying to guess my email address, matthew.paulson@bankofamerica.com would probably be a good place to start. If you guess someone's email address incorrectly, the worst thing that will happen is the message will get returned as undeliverable. You can figure out the format of a particular company's email addresses by doing a web search for the company's domain name followed by

words like "contact' and "email." For example, I
found the email addresses of several Bank of America
employees by searching for "@bankofamerica.com
email."

* **Make an Uneducated Guess** – If you can't figure out
the format of a company's email addresses, you can
also use a service called Email Address Guesser
(guesser.email) to generate probable email addresses
for a person based on their name and their domain
name. You can use a Gmail plugin called Rapportive
(rapportive.com) to figure out if any of the probable
addresses are accurate. After setting up Rapportive in
your browser, open a Gmail account and copy and
paste all of the guesses created by Email Address
Guesser into a new message. Hover over each
address, and the user's other contact information will
appear if the email address is valid. For more
information about how to do this in detail,
UsersThink.com has put together a helpful article
titled "How To Find Someone's Email Address In
Under A Minute"[28], which outlines the process.

* **Use a Paid Service** – There are a number of paid
services that will help you identify someone's email
address based on their name, geographic location, and
the company they work for. Intelius (intelius.com)
and Spokeo (spokeo.com) are two paid services that
have large searchable email address databases. You
can also use business specific search tools like
Data.com (formerly jigsaw.com) and Toofr (toofr.com)
to find the contact information for a specific person at
a business.

Warm Up Your Prospective Customers

Before you begin writing a message to someone, try to find a personal connection with the person you are going to approach. People that you have no connection to at all are known as cold leads. Prospects that have some connection to you or have been referred to you by a mutual acquaintance are considered warm leads. It's much easier to sell to a warm lead than a cold lead, because people have a harder time dismissing those they have an existing personal connection with. If you can turn a cold lead into a warm lead by identifying a mutual friend, acquaintance, or interest, you are much more likely to have success from your introduction email.

In order to identify potential connections with your prospects, look at their Facebook and LinkedIn profiles to see if you have any mutual friends or connections. If you find a mutual connection, ask the connection if they would be willing to introduce you to the prospect through email. If the connection doesn't respond to your request, it's still worthwhile to mention the names of your mutual connection in your introduction email.

If you can't find a personal connection, try to create one through an organization that you are both a member of, such as a university or a service club. If that's not possible, you can try to create a personal connection through a common interest or hobby. Regardless of what kind of connection you create, having some kind of common ground with a prospect will get you a lot further than having no connection at all.

Writing Effective Cold Introduction Emails

After you have identified someone's email address and have figured what kind of personal connection you can make with them, it's time to send them an introduction email. Your introduction email should identify any common bonds that you have with them, let them know how you became aware of them, identify what potential problems they might have that you can help with, and provide a clear call-to-action detailing what next steps you would like them to take.

Here's an example of an introduction email I might send if I were offering consulting services:

Matthew Paulson
To: prospect@marketbeat.com
Subject: Help with your website?

Hi [Name] –

We haven't had the opportunity to meet yet, but I saw you had posted on Twitter that you are looking for a digital marketing expert to help generate more traffic to your website. I wanted to take a moment to introduce myself and see if there's an opportunity for us to work together to do just that.

My company, Matthew Paulson Consulting, works with small- to medium-sized businesses like yours and helps them grow their social media following and collect more email opt-ins with the ultimate goal of driving more sales. We've helped several other [category of business] businesses like yours and think that we could do a lot to grow your audience online.

Would you be available for a phone call tomorrow or the next day to see if there's a way that we can help generate more website traffic and leads for your company?

Feel free to respond to this message or call me on my cell-phone at (605) XXX-XXXX at any time.

Matthew Paulson
Matthew Paulson Consulting

P.S. I saw that we are both connected to John and Jenny Smith on LinkedIn. I went to college with both John and Jenny. They're a great couple. Love those two.

There are several things that you should take note of in this email:

- **Focus on the Prospect** – The content of the message focuses primarily on the prospect and their needs. Start the email by using the person's first name. Use lots of "you" language to make the message more personal, and focus on their specific needs, not what you have to offer.

- **Keep It Short** – The above email is less than two hundred words long. Keep your first introduction email short so that it's easy for the recipient to read. You can dive into detail on how you can help them in a phone call or in a follow-up email.

- **Create a Personal Connection** – At the bottom of this email, I mentioned that we had two mutual connections on LinkedIn. The "P.S." section of your email is a great place to tell someone how you are connected to them without interrupting the flow of your message.

- **Ask for a Next Step** – At the bottom of my email, there is a clear call-to-action for what the next step would be. In most cases, your next step should be getting your prospect on the phone, so you can better qualify them and see if they are a good fit for your services.

- **Use a Relevant and Personal Subject Line** – There's a good chance your prospect's email inbox is already full of other messages. You need to write an intriguing subject line to get your message noticed. Subject lines with a question mark work particularly well. Also use uncommon language that will instill curiosity in the recipient. An example of a subject line that follows these principles is "Strange question?" The subject line is short and will coerce a prospect into opening your message out of curiosity more than anything.

If you are looking for more resources about how to effectively write a cold email, Steli Efti of Close.io created a resource titled "5 cold email templates that will generate warm leads for your sales team!"[29], which provides several great examples of cold emails that get great response rates. John Corcoran has put together another great resource that provides guidance on cold approaching people on the OkDork blog titled "How to Connect with VIPs: 5 Tips for Cold Emails".[30]

Following Up with a Potential Customer

Don't be surprised if you don't receive a response after you send someone a cold email. Some of the most effective cold emails only yield a response rate of 35%. Sometimes people just aren't interested in what you have to offer, and that's okay. Not every prospect is going to become a customer. That doesn't mean you should immediately give up on a prospect if they don't respond to your first email.

It's worthwhile to send one or two follow-up messages in the event that the prospect missed your first message. If you don't receive a response after the follow-ups, your prospect probably just isn't interested, and you should move on to the next one.

Don't send an endless stream of messages asking prospects if they received your email or if they want to get in a phone call with you. When you're emailing someone that hasn't opted into receiving mail from you, you're really crossing over into the territory of spamming if you haven't gotten a positive response after the first contact.

Systemizing the Process

In order to effectively develop your business through email, you are going to need to construct systems and processes to facilitate the process of sending cold emails. You will probably be dealing with many different prospects at once, and many of them will be in different stages. You might have a deal in place with one customer, while at the same time, you are pre-qualifying several more leads and are negotiating contracts with two others. It's important to keep track of where you are with every prospect, so potential customers don't fall through the cracks.

Here are the five stages of turning a prospect into a customer:

- **Pre-qualification** – You think the person has a need, but they have not yet confirmed your suspicions. Prospects that you have emailed but haven't responded are at this stage.

- **Qualification** – You have made contact with a prospective customer, and they have confirmed that they have a need you can meet or a problem you can solve.

- **The Offer** – You make a specific written proposal or offer to address the prospect's need. Your proposal should contain pertinent information about what kind of work you would do for them, including scope of work and pricing.

- **The Contract** – Prospects at this stage have accepted your offer. They sign off on your proposal, complete payment, and become customers of your business.

- **Delivery and Fulfillment** – After you sign an agreement and the customer makes payment, you deliver the product or service you sold them.

The system that you put in place should be able to keep track of where every prospect is at in these five stages. Each prospect should have a next action associated with them, so you know when to take the next step. You can use an advanced contact management system like Contactually (contactually.com) or something as simple as an Excel spreadsheet to keep track of where all of your prospects are at.

Getting Started with Prospecting Through Email

When you first start doing email prospecting, commit to sending five to ten cold emails each week. You can even send these emails through your personal email account because of the low volume outbound of messages.

Each message that you send should be personalized to the recipient and their business. Never send a formal letter. Prospects can recognize generic emails from a mile away.

If someone responds positively to your introduction email, try to set up a phone call or meeting with them to see if you can do business together. If a prospect says they're not interested, move on to the next one.

If someone doesn't respond to your email after four or five days, send them a follow-up email. If they don't respond to your first follow up, you can send one final message if they are a particularly good prospect. If they don't respond to your third message, you should move on to the next prospect.

There are too many fish in the sea to get hung up on one potential customer.

Wrap-Up

Email prospecting can be an incredibly effective strategy for certain types of businesses. If your company sells high price point products and services and you have a relatively small customer base, you should seriously consider whether email prospecting can complement your list-building efforts.

Action Steps

Determine whether inbound email marketing or outbound email marketing is the best approach for your type of business. If you determine that outbound marketing is ideal, complete the steps below:

- Identify the first ten prospective customers you want to approach and find their email addresses.

- Write a sample introduction email that you can use to serve as a template for future cold emails.

- Develop a system to keep track of which step each potential customer is currently in and what your next steps with them are.

- Send your first ten cold emails.

Case Study #5

GoGo Photo Contest

GoGo Photo Contest (gogophotocontest.com) is a company that was founded by Jason Shea, Stevie Shea, and me in July of 2013. The company helps animal shelters and humane societies raise money by running donate-to-vote photo contest fundraisers. GoGo Photo Contest provides software to manage the contest and expertise to promote and market the content in exchange for a percentage of the contest proceeds.

The fundraiser that GoGo Photo Contest helps animal shelters run is a pet photo contest where participants upload pictures of their pets directly to the shelter's contest website. Participants and their friends purchase votes for a donation amount set by the animal welfare group, which is usually $1.00 per vote. Participants will share and promote their entries with their friends through social media and email to get additional votes for their entries. At the end of the contest, the entries that have the most votes will win the contest and get whatever prizes the animal shelter sets for being in the top spot.

GoGo Photo Contest does not rely on traditional inbound email marketing as a marketing channel. Trying to organically grow an audience through traditional list-building methods would not be effective for this business. First of all, GoGo Photo Contest is a relatively new concept, and most decision makers with animal welfare groups aren't searching for photo contest fundraising software. Since many animal welfare groups aren't aware of the concept, most of them would probably never find their way onto our mailing list. Second, there are only approximately 12,000 animal shelters in the United States. This just isn't a big enough set of potential customers to organically grow a mailing list.

It simply wouldn't be effective to use traditional list-building strategies and hope that a meaningful number of animal shelters will sign up for our mailing list and eventually become customers. While inbound email marketing isn't a great fit for GoGo Photo Contest, the company has had great results by doing outbound email marketing and using email as a prospecting tool to identify and market to potential customers. We use many of the principles and strategies outlined in the outbound email marketing chapter of this book to attract customers for GoGo Photo Contest.

Our strategy involves identifying the executive directors of as many animal welfare groups as possible using a variety of different methods. Then, we send a cold email introducing them to GoGo Photo Contest and showing them how our platform can help their organization raise money. Our outreach emails educate our potential customers on the concept of GoGo Photo Contest and suggest they consider it as their next email fundraiser. We will typically send one email per month to an animal shelter director for a few months before we stop mailing them. If a shelter directly responds and tells us they're interested, our team will try to set up a phone call with them in order to sell them on the concept and persuade them to run a contest.

Interestingly enough, GoGo Photo Contest also helps animal welfare groups grow their own email lists. The contests that shelters run are inherently social in nature, and many participants will promote their entries through social media, email, and other word-of-mouth strategies. As a result, many of the people that vote in their contest are not part of any of their constituent lists prior to the beginning of the contest. In addition to the funds raised directly through the contest, the animal shelters have the ability to send follow-up mail and email in the future to solicit additional donations.

GoGo Photo Contest has helped more than 250 different animal shelters run donate-to-vote photo contests primarily because of its outbound email marketing efforts. GoGo Photo Contest's only revenue stream is its share of the proceeds from each contest, which works out to about 9% of the fundraising total. The company has helped shelters raise a total of $1.5 million since the first contest launched in October 2013 and is expected to generate over six figures of revenue in 2015.

Final Thoughts

At the beginning of this book, I argued that email marketing is one of the most powerful marketing channels that companies have available to them. Investing in email as a marketing channel will result in a substantial return-on-investment and will generate dividends for a long period of time. Given the Direct Marketing Association's statistics that the average business investing in email marketing will receive an ROI of 4,300%, any business should salivate over the potential results of incorporating email marketing into their business.

After I heard those numbers the first time, my first thought was, "How can I get this incredibly effective marketing strategy in the hands of my friends and business acquaintances?" I did some digging to find comprehensive resources that would teach all aspects of email marketing, but that book just didn't exist. So, I set out to write one, and *Email Marketing Demystified* is the result. By reading the book, you have learned about all of the key components of email marketing, including learning about email service providers, building a mailing list, creating a lead magnet, setting up an autoresponder series, sending out broadcast emails, writing effective copy, monetizing your list, staying compliant with best practices and government regulations, and doing email prospecting. Now, it's your turn to take the practical knowledge outlined in this book and implement it in your business.

If you haven't already signed up with an email service provider, that's your first step. The next is to start collecting opt-ins on your website using one of many popular plugins. Then, you face the challenge of writing the first few emails in your autoresponder series. In the following several weeks and months, you'll finish your autoresponder series and start writing your first few broadcast emails in hopes of generating some new sales. Over time, your mailing list will grow, you will become a better copywriter, and your sales funnel will become much more effective after trying out different things and seeing what works. If you continue down this path and keep practicing the art of marketing, you will have developed an incredibly powerful skillset that will generate massive results for your business.

Appendix

Additional Email Marketing Resources

If you would like to learn more about how you can grow your business through email marketing, there are several other resources that are worth checking out:

- **AutoResponder Madness**
  (autorespondermadness.com) – AutoResponder
  Madness is an email training course produced by
  Andre Chaperon that teaches marketers to use list
  segmentation and storytelling to create incredibly
  effective autoresponder series that drive engagement
  and sales. I have not personally gone through
  AutoResponder Madness, but it is highly
  recommended by other email marketers that I know
  and trust.

- **Email Players Newsletter** (bensettle.com) – Ben
  Settle's Email Players Newsletter teaches email
  marketers how to write daily entertaining and
  conversational emails to your mailing list. While the
  style of email marketing that Settle promotes isn't
  perfect for everyone, it's hard to recommend an
  expert that knows more about email marketing than
  he.

- **GetResponse's Email Marketing Tips Blog**
  (blog.getresponse.com) – GetResponse publishes a
  daily email marketing tip on its corporate blog. I have
  personally gotten a number of useful ideas by keeping
  up with the content on their blog.

- **MailChimp's Blog** (blog.mailchimp.com) –
  MailChimp regularly publishes email marketing news
  and advice on its corporate blog. Their team regularly
  writes about new ways to attract opt-ins and
  publishes content about trends in the world of email
  marketing.

- **McMethod** (themcmethod.com) – Host John McIntyre
  interviews expert level email marketers who share
  their best tips on his weekly podcast, the McMethod
  Email Marketing Podcast. McIntyre also offers
  professional copywriting services and a membership
  program that provides training videos and sample
  emails which you can use as the basis for messages to
  your mailing list.

- **The Rebel's Guide to Email Marketing** – During the
  last five years, I've read more than a dozen different
  books that cover aspects of email marketing. There are
  a number of mediocre email marketing books that

have been written and a couple of good ones. The *Rebel's Guide to Email Marketing* by DJ Waldow and Jason Falls is one of the best print resources that discusses email marketing (other than *Email Marketing Demystified*, of course).

* **Vero's Email Marketing Blog** (blog.getvero.com) – Vero publishes weekly content about marketing automation on theblog. This blog is focused on more advanced strategies, such as list segmentation and creating triggered email series.

Here are a few other resources that I have produced that you might want to check out:

* **40 Rules for Internet Business Success** – *40 Rules for Internet Business Success* was the first book I published in July 2014. It outlines the 40 principles and strategies that I've used to build a seven-figure business from scratch. You can get your copy of *40 Rules for Internet Business Success* through Amazon at 40RulesBook.com.

* **My Personal Blog** – I regularly publish new business tips and advice on my personal blog at MattPaulson.com.

* **My Podcast Interviews** – While I don't host a podcast of my own, I am regularly a guest on a number of top business podcasts. If you would like to listen to interviews that I've done, visit mattpaulson.com/interviews.

End Notes

1. Radicati, Sara. "Email Statistics Report, 2013-2017." The Radicati Group, Inc. April 2013. http://radicati.com/wp/wp-content/uploads/2013/04/Email-Statistics-Report-2013-2017-Executive-Summary.pdf

2. Clark, Brian. "Email Marketing Essentials." Copyblogger. Rainmaker Digital, LLC. http://copyblogger.com/email-marketing/

3. Deal, David. "Workhorses and dark horses: digital tactics for customer acquisition." GigaOM Research. January 25,2014. http://go.extole.com/rs/extole/images/Gigaom%20Research%20-%20Work%20horses%20and%20dark%20horses.pdf/

4. "Email is not dead. But email IS changing." Marketing Sherpa. Last modified September 2015. http://emailisnotdead.com

5. Lacy, Kyle. "50 Email Marketing Tips and Stats for 2014." ExactTarget. Salesforce, Inc. August 14, 2013. http://exacttarget.com/blog/50-email-marketing-tips-and-stats-for-2014/

6. Beechler, Drew. "75 Digital Marketing Stats from Salesforce Marketing Cloud Research." Salesforce Blog. Salesforce, Inc. November 26, 2014. https://salesforce.com/blog/2014/11/75-digital-marketing-stats-from-salesforce-marketing-cloud-research.html

7. Aufreiter, N., Boudel, J., & Weng, V. "Why marketers should keep sending you e-mails." Insights & Publications. McKinsey & Company. January 2014. http://mckinsey.com/insights/marketing_sales/why_marketers_should_keep_sending_you_emails

8. "SEMPO State of Search Marketing Report 2013." Econsultancy. Econsultancy.com Limited. January 2014. https://econsultancy.com/reports/sempo-state-of-search

9. "United States Internet Users." internet live stats. internetlivestats.com. Last modified July 1, 2014. http://internetlivestats.com/internet-users/united-states/

10. Lacy, Kyle. "50 Email Marketing Tips and Stats for 2014." ExactTarget. Salesforce, Inc. August 14, 2013. http://exacttarget.com/blog/50-email-marketing-tips-and-stats-for-2014/

11. Dvorak, John C. "9 Reasons E-Mail Is Dead." PC Mag online. March 16, 2009. http://pcmag.com/article2/0,2817,2343209,00.asp

12. Wohlsen, Marcus. "The Next Big Thing You Missed: Email's About to Die, Argues Facebook Co-Founder." The Next Big Thing. Wired online. January 21, 2014. http://wired.com/2014/01/next-big-thing-missed-facebook-co-founder-says-email/

13. Brandon, John. "Why Email Will Be Obsolete by 2020." Vision 2020. Inc.com online. April 16, 2015. http://inc.com/john-brandon/why-email-will-be-obsolete-by-2020.html

14. Radicati, Sara. "Email Statistics Report, 2014-2018". The Radicati Group, Inc. April 2014. http://radicati.com/wp/wp-content/uploads/2014/01/Email-Statistics-Report-2014-2018-Executive-Summary.pdf

15. Wiebe, Joanna. "Is the Seemingly Humble Button More Powerful Than the Headline?." Copyhackers. https://copyhackers.com/2014/09/buttons-vs-headlines/

16. Jacobson, Anna. "How Ruben Gamez of Bidsketch Used Drip to Increase Trial Users by 30%." Drip blog. The Numa Group. http://blog.getdrip.com/tips-and-tactics/how-ruben-gamez-of-bidsketch-used-drip-to-increase-trial-users-by-30/

17. "101 Landing Page Optimization Tips." Unbounce. http://unbounce.com/101-landing-page-optimization-tips/

18. "US Consumer Device Preference Report Q1 2014." Movable Ink. http://info.movableink.com/device-report-q1-2014

19. Stec, Carly. "15 Email Newsletter Examples We Love Getting in Our Inboxes." Hubspot blog. Hubspot, Inc. May 8, 2015. https://blog.hubspot.com/marketing/email-newsletter-examples-list

20. Meher, Jessica. "The Ultimate List of 2012 Email Marketing Stats." Hubspot blog. Hubspot, Inc. December 14, 2012. https://blog.hubspot.com/blog/tabid/6307/bid/33901/The-Ultimate-List-of-2012-Email-Marketing-Stats.aspx

21. Admin. "42 Blogging Specialists Explain How to Monetize Email Newsletters and Turn Autoresponder Messages into Profit." AfterOffers Blog. AfterOffers.com. October 2, 2014. http://blog.afteroffers.com/42-blogging-specialists-monetize-email-newsletters/

22. Matthew. "Double Opt-in vs. Single Opt-in Stats." Mailchimp Blog. The Rocket Science Group. September 23, 2011. https://blog.mailchimp.com/double-opt-in-vs-single-opt-in-stats/

23. Bourquin, Tim. "Double Opt-In Is Destroying Your List and Your Business." AfterOffers Blog. AfterOffers.com. April 20, 2015. https://blog.afteroffers.com/double-opt-destroying-your-business/

24. "SendGrid Deliverability Guide: Everything You Need to Know About Delivering Email through Your Web Application." SendGrid. SendGrid.com. http://go.sendgrid.com/rs/sendgrid/images/SendGrid_Deliverability_Guide.pdf

25. ".com Disclosures: How to Make Effective Disclosures in Digital Advertising." Federal Trade Commission. March 2013. https://ftc.gov/sites/default/files/attachments/press-releases/ftc-staff-revises-online-advertising-disclosure-guidelines/130312dotcomdisclosures.pdf

26. "Canada's Anti-Spam Legislation." Government of Canada. Last modified July 9, 2014. http://fightspam.gc.ca/eic/site/030.nsf/eng/00258.html

27. French, Violet A. "Canada's Tough New Anti-Spam Legislation: Beware Its Extra-Territorial Reach." Business Law Today. American Bar Association. January 2014. https://blog.afteroffers.com/double-opt-destroying-your-business/

28. Turner, John. "How To Find Someone's Email Address In Under A Minute." UsersThink. http://usersthink.com/find-email/

29. Efti, Steli. "5 cold email templates that will generate warm leads for your sales team!." Close.io. Elastic, Inc. February 13, 2014. http://blog.close.io/5-cold-email-templates-that-will-generate-warm-leads-for-your-sales-team

30. Corcoran, John. "How to Connect with VIPs: 5 Tips for Cold Emails." OKdork blog. Noah Kagan. July 8, 2014. http://okdork.com/2014/07/08/how-to-email-a-busy-vip-5-tips-for-connecting-with-a-cold-email/

Thank You

Thank you for purchasing *Email Marketing Demystified* and taking the time to read it. Reading a nonfiction book can take quite a bit of time. Thank you for choosing to spend some of your valuable time digging through all the info I have to offer.

If you would like to share your thanks for this book, the best thing you can do is tell a friend about *Email Marketing Demystified* or buy them a copy. I do not have a major publisher or any outside financial backing for this project. The proceeds from every copy sold will go to help my wife, Karine, and I raise our son and pay for his college education.

You can also show your appreciation for this book by leaving a review where you bought it. To leave a review on Amazon, visit the Amazon product page at MyEmailMarketingBook.com. Please be honest with your review and how this book has or has not helped you on your path to building an Internet business. I want everyone to know how or if this book has changed your life in any significant way.

You can follow me online at my personal blog, MattPaulson.com. You can also follow me on Twitter (@MatthewDP).

If we have met in real life, feel free to add me as a friend on Facebook (facebook.com/matthewpaulson). If we have not met in real life, you are still welcome to "follow" me on Facebook.

I am also on LinkedIn (linkedin.com/in/matthewpaulson) and AngelList (angel.co/matthewpaulson).

If you would like to hear me talk about various topics, feel free to check out the interviews I have done at mattpaulson.com/interviews.

Thanks again and God Bless,

Matthew Paulson
October 1, 2015

Acknowledgements

I would like to express my sincere gratitude to my many friends, family members, and business acquaintances that have encouraged me while I have pursued various entrepreneurial adventures over the last decade.

I would like to thank my wife, Karine, for being incredibly supportive, putting up with my unusual work schedule, and trusting me to provide for our family through my business.

I would like to thank my three-year-old son, Micah, for the many smiles he puts on my face each day.

I would like to thank my business partners and team members, including David Anicetti, Donna Helling, Todd Kolb, Don Miller, Tyler Prins, Rebecca McKeever, Jason Shea, Stevie Shea, and Toi Williams. Without them, my companies would not be where they are today.

Finally, I would like to express my gratitude to the many talented people that worked on this book.

I would like to thank John McIntyre for writing the foreword of this book.

I would like to thank Elisa Doucette and her team for editing this book and fixing my many grammar and spelling errors.

I would like to thank Ellen Jesperson for designing the cover of this book.

I would like to thank James Woosley for doing this book's layout.

I would like to thank Stu Gray and Toby Lyles for putting together the audio version of this book.

I would like to thank Tom Morkes and Perrin Carrell for helping promote this book.

About the Author

Matthew Paulson is a serial entrepreneur if there ever was one. His largest business, MarketBeat.com (formerly Analyst Ratings Network), publishes a financial newsletter to more than 250,000 investors on a daily basis. He is also a partner at GoGo Photo Contest, a company that helps animal welfare groups raise money through donate-to-vote photo contest fundraisers. Finally, he is a partner at USGolfTV, which is a digital publishing company that produces a regionally syndicated television show and other content for the golf industry.

Matthew holds a B.S. in Computer Science and an M.S. in Information Systems from Dakota State University. He also holds an M.A. in Christian Leadership from Sioux Falls Seminary.

Matthew's first book, *40 Rules for Internet Business Success*, shared the principles and strategies that he's used to build a seven-figure Internet business (and multiple six-figure businesses) from scratch. Matthew's second book, *Email Marketing Demystified*, provides a step-by-step guide for any entrepreneur to implement email marketing in their business.

Matthew resides in Sioux Falls, South Dakota, where he lives with his wonderful wife, Karine, and his adorable son, Micah.

Connect with Matthew at:

- Matthew's Personal Blog - MattPaulson.com
- AngelList - angel.co/matthewpaulson
- Facebook - facebook.com/matthewpaulson
- LinkedIn - LinkedIn.com/in/matthewpaulson
- Twitter - twitter.com/matthewdp
- Email - matt@mattpaulson.com